A VINDICATION OF
NATURAL SOCIETY

EDMUND BURKE

A VINDICATION OF NATURAL SOCIETY

*OR, A VIEW OF
THE MISERIES AND EVILS
ARISING TO MANKIND
FROM EVERY SPECIES OF
ARTIFICIAL SOCIETY.*

*IN A LETTER TO LORD * * * *
BY A LATE NOBLE WRITER.*

Edmund Burke

*Edited and with an introduction by
Frank N. Pagano*

INDIANAPOLIS

LibertyClassics is a publishing imprint of Liberty Fund, Inc., a foundation established to encourage study of the ideal of a society of free and responsible individuals.

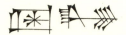

The cuneiform inscription that serves as the design motif for our endpapers is the earliest known written appearance of the word "freedom" (ama-gi), or liberty. It is taken from a clay document written about 2300 B.C. in the Sumerian city-state of Lagash.

Frontispiece and cover art courtesy of Prof. William F. Campbell.

Library of Congress Cataloging in Publication Data

Burke, Edmund, 1729?–1797.
    A vindication of natural society.

    Includes index.
    1. State, The.   2. Natural law.   I. Pagano,
Frank N.   II. Title.
JC176.B8287 1982   320.1   81–84826
ISBN 0–86597–009–2   AACR2
ISBN 0–86597–010–6 (pbk.)

10 9 8 7 6 5 4 3 2 1

CONTENTS

NOTE ON THE TEXT

*I*n order that the *Vindication* may be read as Burke intended it, I have followed, as much as possible, the text of the second, revised edition of 1757. Burke's notes are indicated by an asterisk and appear at the bottom of the page.

My notes are indicated by a number and also appear at the bottom of the page. My notes have several purposes. They supply historical information on the persons and events mentioned in the text. They identify textual curiosities and allusions to other works, translate quotations, and indicate their original sources.

The variants are found in the back of the volume and are identified by a letter. All variants, with one exception, are from the 1756 first edition. The exception is from the 1757 edition and appears to be a printer's error which makes the text unintelligible and therefore was relegated to the variants. Included among the variants is the "Advertisement" to the first edition.

I am grateful to Harvard University for the opportunity to consult from its rare book collection in Houghton Library the first, second, and third editions of the *Vindication*. The facsimile of the title page from the second edition is reproduced by permission of the Houghton Library, Harvard University.

I would like to thank J. Brian Benestad for translating several of the *Vindication*'s Latin quotations and the following publishers for permission to reproduce passages from the works indicated: Random House, Inc., The Modern Library (trans. Christian E. Detmold, Machiavelli's *Discourses on the First Ten Books of Titus Livius*); Encyclopedia Britannica (trans. James Rhoades, Virgil's *Georgic* II); Elsevier-Dutton, Co., Inc., Everyman's Library (Hobbes's *Leviathan*); Harvard University Press (trans. M. Hutton, rev. R.M. Ogilivie, Tacitus' *Agricola*; trans. G.G. Ramsay, Juvenal's *Satire VI*; trans. W.A. Falconer, Cicero's *De amicitia*; and trans. Bernadotte Perrin, Plutarch's *Lives*); and St. Martin's Press (trans. Roger Masters and Judith Masters. Rousseau's *Second Discourse*).

FRANK N. PAGANO

INTRODUCTION

I

*E*dmund Burke described the French Revolution as "the most astonishing [crisis] that has
hitherto happened in the world."[1] On nothing
did it have a more astonishing effect than on his
reputation. Because the French Revolution drew
new political lines and fixed in its aftermath the
political vocabulary even until the present, as its
implacable foe, Burke has come down to us as the
foremost conservative in the English-speaking
world. Yet he called himself an Old Whig.

There were no conservatives and no liberals
before the Revolution.[2] Burke, the late eighteenth-
century Whig, certainly would have found himself more at home in the nineteenth-century
Conservative Party, the party of the Tories, than in
the nineteenth-century Whig Party, which eventually merged with the Liberal Party. There are two

---

[1]*The Works of Edmund Burke,* 12 vols. (Boston: Little, Brown & Co.,
1899), 3:243–44.

[2]*Ibid.,* 4:68–69.

simple explanations of Burke's attitude toward the Revolution and its redesigning of the political map: 1. He changed his opinions with the appearance of the revolutionary tear in civilization. The French Revolution led him to become conservative contrary to his old principles; 2. The Revolution was utterly new. Consistent with his ancient principles, he opposed it, and his former allies, consistent or inconsistent with theirs, supported it.[3] At stake in this controversy is more than the consistency of Burke's political thought. Involved also are the intellectual respectabilities of those conservatives, who, following him, have resisted the revolutionary movements of modern history.

II

Burke's life was a weave of contraries. Born in 1729 of an Irish Protestant father and an Irish

---

[3] A complete list of even the major Burke scholarship would require a bibliography of considerable length. The predominant view of Burke runs in cycles. The last group of studies considered him inconsistent. See, for example, Michael Freeman, *Edmund Burke and the Critique of Political Radicalism* (Chicago: University of Chicago Press, 1980); Frederick Dreyer, *Burke's Politics* (Waterloo, Ontario: Wilfred Laurier University Press, 1979); and Isaac Kramnick, *The Rage of Edmund Burke* (New York: Basic Books, 1977). The previous group of studies, in contrast, contended that Burke was consistent. See Francis Canavan, *The Political Reason of Edmund Burke* (Durham, N.C.: Duke University Press, 1960); Peter Stanlis, *Edmund Burke and Natural Law* (Ann Arbor, Mich.: University of Michigan Press, 1958); Charles Parkin, *The Moral Basis of Burke's Political Thought* (London: Cambridge University Press, 1956); and Leo Strauss, *Natural Right and History* (Chicago: University of Chicago Press, 1953), pp. 294–323.

Catholic mother, he was educated to follow his father into law. During the expected culmination of that education at London's Middle Temple, he turned away from law and drifted into a temporary obscurity. The publication of his first work, *A Vindication of Natural Society*, in 1756, signaled his emergence from that period and the beginning of his literary career. Within two years, he published *A Philosophical Inquiry into the Origin of Our Ideas of the Sublime and Beautiful*, revised the *Vindication*, and became the primary editor of the *Annual Register*, a review of the year's events, discoveries, and publications. In 1759 he acquired a political patron, William Hamilton, but after six years, he bitterly dissolved his ties to Hamilton because he wanted Burke to suspend his literary activities. Paradoxically, 1765 was the year in which Burke's literary career ended, except for the writing of practical tracts. He stopped his editing of the *Annual Register* and accepted the position as private secretary to the great Whig lord, the Marquis of Rockingham, whom the king had made Prime Minister. Burke entered the House of Commons, where he was a fixture for the next thirty years.

It was his parliamentary career and its associated writings on political affairs that won Burke his reputation. They provide, as well, the evidence of his apparent inconsistency. The unremitting enemy of the French Revolution from 1790 to his death, in 1797, supported the American Revolution in the decade of the seventies. The author of *Reflections on the Revolution in France* (1790) and *An Appeal from the New to the Old Whigs* (1791), to some, seems to have argued against the author of the *Speech on American Taxation* (1774) and the *Speech on Conciliation with America* (1775). The statesman, who fashioned the Whig Party into the model of all modern political parties, tore his handiwork to bits when it threatened to be the instrument by which the French Revolution might be introduced into the domestic politics of Britain. The prosecutor for nine years (1786–1795) of Warren Hastings, whom Burke accused of conquering India by force and fraud, refused to accept the smallest dismantling of the so-called rotten boroughs by which the aristocracy controlled the membership and thence the votes in the House of Commons. The lonely advocate of the enfranchisement of the Irish Catholics fought the extension of the ballot in England. Upon retirement, in 1795, the champion of prescription, in defense of his own pension, wrote *A Letter to a Noble Lord*, a polemic against undeserved aristocratic privilege. Throughout Burke maintained that he was consistent and right.

III

Although the *Vindication* is the only purely theoretical consideration of politics that Burke ever wrote, the search for his principles has normally entailed the painstaking compilation of the opinions found in his diverse writings on the practical issues that he confronted in his parliamentary labors. Yet his practical works, especially the anti-revolutionary tracts, which earned him his conservative reputation, may be a poor place to seek the grounds of his conservatism. In the anti-revolutionary works, for example, he tried to confine to France not only the Revolution but also its source. He understood the Revolution to have originated in a literary cabal that included several significant French philosophers. He denied, during the Revolution, that either the French or the comparable British group had any lasting influence on British public affairs. He was surely right about the Britons he names in the *Reflections*. The single significant writer he could dismiss with the questions, "Who now reads Bolingbroke? Who ever read him through?"[4] The *Reflections* is silent about the two major British thinkers, Thomas Hobbes

---

[4]*Works of Edmund Burke,* 3:349.

and John Locke, who probably influenced both the French revolutionary philosophers and the Old Whigs. The *Vindication*, however, speaks of Hobbes and Locke and implicitly links them to Henry St. John, Viscount Bolingbroke, and his friend, Alexander Pope. It alludes to Charles Montesquieu and Jean Jacques Rousseau. Of all Burke's works, only his first considers directly the effects of the enlightenment thinkers on the British constitution.

The *Vindication* is not a straightforward work of political theory. Although Burke's political thought may appear only there in one compact formulation, it is not of easy access, for he puts between himself and his audience a fictional author. The work was published anonymously as a letter attributed by the title page to "a late noble writer." In the preface to the second revised edition (1757), Burke identified Bolingbroke as one of a group of men that he imitated or parodied. That Burke ever intended to convince the reading public that Bolingbroke was the true author of the *Vindication* is doubtful. One of the first reviews of it saw through the ruse and revealed that its author was a student at the Temple.[5] Almost immediately there arose another dispute that has persisted: was the *Vindication* a satire of

---

[5]*Critical Review*, June 1756, p. 400.

Bolingbroke or was it a serious exposition of the young Burke's political thought? The arguments followed the lines of Burke scholarship. Those who maintained that he was a consistent conservative read the *Vindication* as a *reductio ad absurdum* of the arguments of Bolingbroke and his rationalist brethren.[6] Others, who sought confirmation of Burke's inconsistency, found too much true passion in the piece for it to be chiefly a satire.[7] To them, Burke in his most youthful work wrote most radically. Age eroded his radicalism until he was transformed into the mouthpiece of the rich and powerful.

IV

The controversy surrounding the *Vindication* thus involves a fundamental question of interpretation: is it a satire or a serious tract? Perhaps the

[6]*Monthly Review,* July 1756, pp. 18–22; T.E. Utley, *Edmund Burke* (London: Longmans, Green & Co., 1957), pp. 16–17; John C. Weston, Jr., "The Ironic Purpose of Burke's *Vindication* Vindicated," *Journal of the History of Ideas,* 19 (June 1958): 435–41; Peter Stanlis, ed., *Edmund Burke: Selected Writings and Speeches* (Garden City, New York: Doubleday & Co., 1963), pp. 40–41; and Frank O'Gorman, *Edmund Burke: His Political Philosophy* (Bloomington, Indiana: Indiana University Press, 1973), pp. 17–19.

[7]William Godwin, *Enquiry Concerning Political Justice and its Influences on Morals and Happiness,* 3 vols. (Toronto: University of Toronto Press, 1946), 1:13, note; 2:545–46, note; J.B. Bury, *The Idea of Progress* (London: MacMillan & Co., 1928), pp. 181–82; Elie Halevy, *The Growth of Philosophic Radicalism* (London: Faber and Faber, 1934), pp. 215–16; Murray Rothbard, "A Note on Burke's *A Vindication of Natural Society,*" *Journal of the History of Ideas,* 19 (Jan. 1958): 114–18; and Kramnick, pp. 88–89.

best guide to how the piece should be read is the preface to the second edition. According to this preface, the work imitates and does not imitate the writings of Bolingbroke. It adopts his method of writing "sometimes concealed, sometimes openly and fully" (p. 5), but it contains an "under-plot of more consequence" (p. 9) than the mere imitating or parodying of him. If we accept the suggestions of the preface, then, the *Vindication* is emphatically not a treatise of political philosophy. Whatever philosophy it espouses comes to light in the words and plot of a fictional letter from an anonymous noble writer to an anonymous young lord. Burke is both and neither the noble writer and the young lord. He authors all the noble writer's words and arouses all the passions of the noble writer and the young lord, but their characters and the plot may compel him to write lies, or they may allow him to write noble lies. Indeed the fictional form permits Burke flagrantly to place before the public unpopular or terrible truths, which most readers will regard as only belonging to the fictional noble writer and not to the real author. Therefore, while the whole *Vindication* may tell the truth, some of its parts may be false, but its false parts may not be those that the reader believes to be so.

The fictional, noble writer has a purpose for writing the letter. He acts to persuade the young man not to repeat errors that the older and dying man has committed. His advice is to avoid politics. In the course of defending his advice, he returns to the foundations of society, and from that perspective, he condemns all the civil societies of all times. We learn from him that in a conversation on the same subject, previous to the letter but cut off at its beginning, the young lord allowed the noble writer's principle but expressed the fear that their speculations might lead to a total condemnation of society. Thus, however one might prefer the conservatism of the young lord or the radicalism of the noble writer, both agree on two items: 1. The search for the foundations of society leads back to the state of nature; 2. That return may subvert all civil society.

The return to the state of nature is a trek taken first by Hobbes, then by Locke, and, we may say, finally by Rousseau, because he did it so completely. The *Vindication* begins with the assumption that informed classical liberalism: man was in the state of nature. Society is neither divine nor natural but artificial. The letter supposedly vindicates natural society (Bolingbroke's phrase[8]), but it is

---

[8]Henry St. John, Viscount Bolingbroke, *The Philosophical Writings of the Late Henry St. John, Viscount Bolingbroke,* 5 vols. (London: David Mallet, 1754), 4:41–43, 46, 53.

striking that this society is referred to only three times and described but once. The state of nature is mentioned twelve times, and aspects of it are described throughout the letter. Natural society is not man's original condition. Originally he was in the state of nature. Natural society is a short stopover between the state of nature and civil society. So much of the letter perplexes that it is not surprising that in no obvious way does the noble writer vindicate natural society. Nor does he fix his conception of the state of nature. In some parts of the letter, he depicts it as an inconvenient state where men want, think, and act as men do in civil society. Elsewhere he envisions it as an idyllic state where men do not think at all and do not want beyond easy natural satisfaction. The protean character of his description of the state of nature allows him to attack the whole variety of governments and societies. But not even by implication does the letter assert that the foundations of society are to be sought otherwise than in a return to the state of nature. There is no alternative to the method of the liberal philosophers unless the foundations of society should not be sought at all.

Although the two characters agree on some points, the young lord disputes the noble writer's contention that if society cannot be rationally justified, it ought to be abandoned. The noble writer observes that the young lord would argue that given the current human condition, civil society is necessary. The younger man did not have the same conservative attitude toward revealed or artificial religion. The preface claims that the work's design was to show that the method of attack used against revealed religion can also be used against civil society. This truth the noble writer knows. It is the young lord who did not realize that the assaults on religion could be related to the critique of all government. He was not hesitant to attack religion.

If the young lord holds fast to his conviction that civil society is necessary, then for him, the letter is a defense of religion. The noble writer again and again contends that civil society cannot stand without an artificial religion. Not that artificial religion is true—to the contrary. Because civil society has its foundations laid on falsehoods, it needs the support of a false religion. Should the young lord reject the older man's advice to escape civil society and should he continue to insist on entering politics, then the noble writer recommends hypocrisy: appear to adhere to the popular religion.

There is no clear description of the popular religion (or, for that matter, the natural religion of the noble writer). The best assumption is that it is Christianity. Sprinkled about are hints that it may also include a measure of popular philosophy—

perhaps the natural rights philosophy of Locke (p. 43). Modernity may have already invaded the popular conscience, and anyone entering politics must appear to adhere to a jumble of philosophy and prejudice. The noble writer scolds the young lord for this desire to be inconsistent. In any case, the defense of religion rests on the grounds of its usefulness to civil society.

V

The foregoing does not dispose of the enduring controversy of whether the *Vindication* ultimately is satirical or serious, wise or foolish. According to the preface, Burke took great pains to make his first piece a work of concealment. If it is consistent with the principles of his later works, some of the confusion attending them perhaps stems from his reluctance to expose his principles to public scrutiny. Burke's thought freely flaunted may be as menacing to civil society as that of the wildest enlightenment thinker. In some ways, even the replacement of the advertisement to the first edition by the preface to the second may have increased the difficulty of reading the *Vindication*. The former raises a fundamental question about the work's plot: how did the letter find its way into print? The advertisement admits that the noble writer did not intend the letter to be published. Therefore, the young lord perhaps conveyed it to the editor (or was the editor). Was he persuaded? And persuaded of what? Or did he conclude that this letter, as an extravagant example of abusive enlightenment thinking, ought to be given to the public to alert it to the gathering dangers posed by the bulk of these writings? Fortunately, introductions may raise questions without answering them.

FRANK N. PAGANO

A VINDICATION OF
NATURAL SOCIETY

PREFACE[a]

*B*efore the Philosophical Works of Lord Bolingbroke[1] had appeared, great Things were expected from the Leisure of a Man, who from the splendid Scene of Action, in which his Talents had enabled him to make so conspicuous a Figure, had retired to employ those Talents in the Investigation of Truth. Philosophy began to congratulate herself upon such a Proselyte from the World of Business, and hoped to have extended her Power under the Auspices of such a Leader. In the Midst of these pleasing Expectations, the Works themselves at last appeared in *full Body*, and with great Pomp. Those who searched in them for new Discoveries in the Mys-

---

[1]Henry St. John, Viscount Bolingbroke (1678–1751) was an English statesman who rose under Harley to become a Secretary of State for Queen Anne and negotiated the treaty of Utrecht (1713). When George I succeeded to the throne and installed a Whig ministry under Walpole, Bolingbroke, threatened by impeachment, fled to France, returned, fled again, and finally settled in Britain only after Walpole's departure from politics. When in Britain, Bolingbroke used a new journal, the *Craftsman*, to oppose the Whigs. His *Philosophical Works* (5 vols. [London: 1754]) were published posthumously by David Mallet. The Viscount was also a

teries of Nature; those who expected something which might explain or direct the Operations of the Mind; those who hoped to see Morality illustrated and enforced; those who looked for new Helps to Society and Government; those who desired to see the Characters and Passions of Mankind delineated; in short, all who consider such Things as Philosophy, and require some of them at least, in every philosophical Work, all these were certainly disappointed; they found the Land-marks of Science precisely in their former Places: And they thought they received but a poor Recompence for this Disappointment, in seeing every Mode of Religion attacked in a lively Manner, and the Foundation of every Virtue, and of all Government, sapped with great Art and much Ingenuity. What Advantage do we derive from

---

friend of Alexander Pope who began his *Essay on Man* with an exhortation for St. John to awake.

A large body of criticism assumes that the noble writer of the *Vindication* is a caricature of Bolingbroke and the work merely a satire of his philosophy. Bolingbroke scholars, however, contend that the *Vindication*'s arguments are not a close representation of his philosophy. See Walter Sichel, *Bolingbroke and His Times*, 2 vols. (New York: Haskell House Publishers, 1968), 2:439–447; and J.B. Cressman, "Burke's Satire on Bolingbroke in *A Vindication of Natural Society*," (Ph.D. Diss., University of Michigan, 1958). In fact, the name, Lord Bolingbroke, never appears in the body of the *Vindication* and only appears three times in the preface (pp. 3, 5, 10). The anonymous editor, who writes the preface, does refer to Bolingbroke as "this noble writer" (p. 5) but goes on to associate him with "several others." He belongs to a group of writers, all of whom may have a part in the character and philosophy of the *Vindication*'s noble writer. Among these writers probably are those modern philosophers explicitly and implicitly referred to in the work.

such Writings? What Delight can a Man find in employing a Capacity which might be usefully exerted for the noblest Purposes, in a sort of sullen Labour, in which, if the Author could succeed, he is obliged to own, that nothing could be more fatal to Mankind than his Success?

I cannot conceive how this sort of Writers propose to compass the Designs they pretend to have in view, by the Instruments which they employ. Do they pretend to exalt the Mind of Man, by proving him no better than a Beast? Do they think to enforce the Practice of Virtue, by denying that Vice and Virtue are distinguished by good or ill Fortune here, or by Happiness or Misery hereafter? Do they imagine they shall increase our Piety, and our Reliance on God, by exploding his Providence, and insisting that he is neither just nor good? Such are the Doctrines which, sometimes concealed, sometimes openly and fully avowed, are found to prevail throughout the Writings of Lord Bolingbroke; and such are the Reasonings which this noble Writer and several others have been pleased to dignify with the Name of Philosophy. If these are delivered in a specious Manner, and in a Stile above the common, they cannot want a Number of Admirers of as much Docility as can be wished for in Disciples. To these the Editor of the following little Piece has addressed it: there is no Reason to conceal the Design of it any longer.

The Design was, to shew that, without the Exertion of any considerable Forces, the same Engines which were employed for the Destruction of Religion, might be employed with equal Success for the Subversion of Government; and that specious Arguments might be used against those Things which they, who doubt of every thing else, will never permit to be questioned. It is an Observation which I think *Isocrates* makes in one of his Orations against the Sophists,[2] That it is far more easy to maintain a wrong Cause, and to support paradoxical Opinions to the Satisfaction of a common Auditory, than to establish a doubtful Truth by solid and conclusive Arguments. When Men find that something can be said in favour of

---

[2]Isocrates (436–338 B.C.) was an Athenian orator and a student of the philosopher Socrates. The argument the editor paraphrases is not found in the oration, *Against the Sophists*, although there is one by that title, but in the *Antidosis*. An antidosis was a trial in which the defendant sought to prove himself too poor to undertake the expense of a Greek warship. After losing such a trial, Isocrates composed the *Antidosis* to defend his life's devotion to wisdom. Its arguments are very similar to those found in Plato's *Apology of Socrates*.

The specific argument referred to above is made by Isocrates to his student, the Athenian general Timotheus. See *Isocrates II*, trans. George Norlin and LaRue Van Hook (Cambridge, Mass.: Harvard University Press, 1968), pp. 262–264. The orator points out that in Athens political success depends upon flattering the demagogues. The logic of the observation suggests that Timotheus should either flatter them, something both he and Isocrates admit is dishonorable, or abandon politics, an act which would have been a serious loss for the city. Timotheus eventually was forced to flee Athens and died in exile.

what, on the very Proposal, they have thought utterly indefensible, they grow doubtful of their own Reason; they are thrown into a sort of pleasing Surprize; they run along with the Speaker, charmed and captivated to find such a plentiful Harvest of Reasoning, where all seemed barren and unpromising. This is the Fairy Land of Philosophy. And it very frequently happens, that those pleasing Impressions on the Imagination, subsist and produce their Effect, even after the Understanding has been satisfied of their unsubstantial Nature. There is a sort of Gloss upon ingenious Falsehoods, that dazzles the Imagination, but which neither belongs to, nor becomes the sober Aspect of Truth. I have met with a Quotation in Lord *Coke*'s Reports that pleased me very much, though I do not know from whence he has taken it: "*Interdum fucata falsitas,* [says he] *in multis est probabilior, et sæpe rationibus vincit nudam veritatem.*"[3] In such Cases, the Writer has a certain

---

[3]"Occasionally invented falsehood in many things is more probable and often by reasons conquers the naked truth." (Trans. J. Brian Benestad.) Sir Edward Coke (1552–1634) was an English jurist and chief justice of the king's bench. The *Reports* are commentaries on decisions in common law which took pains to emphasize the consistency of all decisions with ancient principles. He was notorious for manufacturing Latin quotations defending his position and then claiming that they were ancient maxims or rules of law. The editor implies that this quotation is an example of such an invented maxim. Although it may well appear in one of the volumes of the *Reports,* I was unable to find it. It is possible that the anonymous editor himself constructed it and, employing Coke's own method, falsely attributed it to the *Reports.*

Fire and Alacrity inspired into him by a Consciousness, that let it fare how it will with the Subject, his Ingenuity will be sure of Applause; and this Alacrity becomes much greater if he acts upon the offensive, by the Impetuosity that always accompanies an Attack, and the unfortunate Propensity which Mankind have to the finding and exaggerating Faults. The Editor is satisfied that a Mind which has no Restraint from a Sense of its own Weakness, of its subordinate Rank in the Creation, and of the extreme Danger of letting the Imagination loose upon some Subjects may very plausibly attack every thing the most excellent and venerable; that it would not be difficult to criticise the Creation itself; and that if we were to examine the divine Fabricks by our Ideas of Reason and Fitness, and to use the same Method of Attack by which some Men have assaulted Revealed Religion, we might with as good Colour, and with the same Success, make the Wisdom and Power of God in his Creation appear to many no better than Foolishness. There is an Air of Plausibility which accompanies vulgar Reasonings and Notions taken from the beaten Circle of ordinary Experience, that is admirably suited to the narrow Capacities of some, and to the Laziness of others. But this Advantage is in great measure lost, when a painful, comprehensive Survey of a very complicated Matter, and which requires a great Variety of Considerations, is to be made; when we must seek in a profound Subject, not only for Arguments, but for new Materials of Argument, their Measures and their Method of Arrangement; when we must go out of the Sphere of our ordinary Ideas, and when we can never walk sure but by being sensible of our Blindness. And this we must do, or we do nothing, whenever we examine the Result of a Reason which is not our own. Even in Matters which are, as it were, just within our Reach, what would become of the World if the Practice of all moral Duties, and the Foundations of Society, rested upon having their Reasons made clear and demonstrative to every Individual?

The Editor knows that the Subject of this Letter is not so fully handled as obviously it might; it was not his Design to say all that could possibly be said.[4] It had been inexcusable to fill a large Volume with the Abuse of Reason; nor would such an Abuse have been tolerable even for a few Pages, if some Under-plot, of more Consequence

---

[4]This is the only place in the preface where the editor partly drops his disguise and admits that he is the author of the piece. He never, however, identifies himself as Edmund Burke. Moreover, this dropping of the fictional veil immediately precedes the more startling revelation that even the preface does not entirely expose the "Under-plot, of more Consequence than the apparent Design" described on p. 6.

than the apparent Design, had not been carried on.

Some Persons have thought that the Advantages of the State of Nature ought to have been more fully displayed. This had undoubtedly been a very ample Subject for Declamation; but they do not consider the Character of the Piece. The Writers against Religion, whilst they oppose every System, are wisely careful never to set up any of their own. If some Inaccuracies in Calculation, in Reasoning, or in Method be found, perhaps these will not be looked upon as Faults by the Admirers of Lord Bolingbroke; who will, the Editor is afraid, observe much more of his Lordship's Character in such Particulars of the following Letter, than they are like to find of that rapid Torrent of an impetuous and overbearing Eloquence, and the Variety of rich Imagery for which that Writer is justly admired.

A LETTER TO LORD****

*S*hall I venture to say, my Lord, that in our late Conversation, you were inclined to the Party which you adopted rather by the Feelings of your good Nature, than by the Conviction of your Judgment? We laid open the Foundations of Society; and you feared, that the Curiosity of this Search might endanger the Ruin of the whole Fabrick. You would readily have allowed my Principle, but you dreaded the Consequences; you thought, that having once entered upon these Reasonings, we might be carried insensibly and irresistably farther than at first we could either have imagined or wished. But for my part, my Lord, I then thought, and am still of the same Opinion, that Error, and not Truth of any kind, is dangerous; that ill Conclusions can only flow from false Propositions; and that, to know whether any Proposition be true or false, it is a preposterous Method to examine it by its apparent Consequences.

These were the Reasons which induced me to go so far into that Enquiry; and they are the Reasons which direct me in all my Enquiries. I had indeed often reflected on that Subject before I could prevail upon myself to communicate my Reflections to any body. They were generally melancholy enough; as those usually are which carry us beyond the mere Surface of Things; and which would undoubtedly make the Lives of all thinking Men extremely miserable, if the same Philosophy which caused the Grief, did not at the same Time administer the Comfort.

On considering political Societies, their Origin, their Constitution, and their Effects, I have sometimes been in a good deal more than Doubt, whether the Creator did ever really intend Man for a State of Happiness. He has mixed in his Cup a Number of natural Evils,[5] (in spite of the Boasts of Stoicism[6] they are Evils) and every Endeavor

---

[5]This is the first use of the word "Evils." Despite the alternative title, the *Vindication* first associates evils with nature. Miseries, however, are always associated with artificial society. Compare Rousseau's understanding of misery, *The First and Second Discourses*, ed. Roger Masters, trans. Roger Masters and Judith Masters (New York: St. Martin's Press, 1964), pp. 127–28.

[6]The Stoics were members of an ancient philosophical school, founded by Zeno of Citium (c.334–c.262). They met in the Stoa Poecile (painted porch) where Zeno lectured. The Stoics thought that to be happy is to practice virtue and that pleasure and pain do not truly effect happiness. See Epictetus, *Encheirdon,* or Marcus Aurelius, *Meditations.* For an understanding of the Stoics contemporary to Burke and the one which he may have had in mind as he wrote, see Charles Montesquieu, *The Spirit of the Laws,* Bk. 24, ch. 10.

which the Art and Policy of Mankind has used
from the Beginning of the World to this Day, in
order to alleviate, or cure them, has only served to
introduce new Mischiefs, or to aggravate and inflame the old. Besides this, the Mind of Man itself
is too active and restless a Principle ever to settle
on the true Point of Quiet. It discovers every Day
some craving Want in a Body, which really wants
but little. It every Day invents some new artificial
Rule to guide that Nature which if left to itself
were the best and surest Guide. It finds out imaginary Beings prescribing imaginary Laws; and
then, it raises imaginary Terrors to support a Belief in the Beings, and an Obediance to the Laws.
Many Things have been said, and very well undoubtedly, on the Subjection in which we should
preserve our Bodies to the Government of our
Understanding; but enough has not been said
upon the Restraint which our bodily Necessities

The reference to the Stoics marks the introduction of the influence of
a competing school of ancient philosophy, the Epicurean, named after its
founder Epicurus (341–271). Epicureanism, in contrast to Stoicism, is a
form of hedonism. According to it, happiness is found in the pleasure of
contemplation and the avoidance of pain and political cares. The cup,
which the noble writer pictures as the place where the Creator mixes the
components of human fate, is an allusion to the poem of the Roman
Epicurean, Lucretius, *De rerum natura,* Bk. 1, lines 248–51; Bk. 4, lines
1–25. Lucretius employs the image of the cup to explain the nature of his
poetic art. Like a physician, he has mixed the honey of his words with
the wormwood of his Epicurean philosophy. The poet fills the cup and
slowly reveals the evils of nature. For Burke's evaluation of *De rerum
natura,* and Epicureanism, see *The Works of Edmund Burke,* 12 vols. (Boston: Little, Brown & Co., 1899), 7:251.

ought to lay on the extravagant Sublimities, and
excentrick Rovings of our Minds. The Body, or as
some love to call it, our inferior Nature, is wiser in
its own plain Way, and attends its own Business
more directly than the Mind with all its boasted
Subtilty.

In the State of Nature,[7] without question, Mankind was subjected to many and great Incon-
veniencies. Want of Union, Want of mutual Assistance, Want of a common Arbitrator to resort to in
their Differences. These were Evils which they
could not but have felt pretty severely on many
Occasions. The original Children of the Earth
lived with their Brethren of the other Kinds in
much Equality. Their Diet must have been
confined almost wholly to the vegetable Kind;
and the same Tree, which in its flourishing State
produced them Berries, in its Decay gave them an
Habitation. The mutual Desires of the Sexes unit-
ing their Bodies and Affections, and the Children,[a] which were the Results of these Inter-
courses, introduced first the Notion of Society,
and taught its Conveniences. This Society,
founded in natural Appetites and Instincts, and

---

[7]Including the preface, the phrase, "State of Nature," appears, I believe, twelve times. The noble writer does not describe the state consis-
tently. Its first description acknowledges that it had evils and inconveniences, reminiscent of Locke's depiction of it. See *The Second Treatise
of Government*, chs. 2 and 3. Compare also the preface of the *Vindication*,
p. 10.

not in any positive Institution, I shall call *Natural Society*.[8] Thus far Nature went, and succeeded; but Man would go farther. The great Error of our Nature is, not to know where to stop, not to be satisfied with any reasonable Acquirement; not to compound with our Condition; but to lose all we have gained by an insatiable Pursuit after more. Man found a considerable Advantage by this Union of many Persons to form one Family; he therefore judged that he would find his Account proportionably in an Union of many Families into one Body politick. And as Nature has formed no Bond of Union to hold them together, he supplied this Defect by *Laws*.

This is *Political Society*.[9] And hence the Sources of what are usually called States, civil Societies, or Governments; into some Form of which, more extended or restrained, all Mankind have gradually fallen. And since it has so happened, and that we

---

[8]The term, "Natural Society," occurs but three times in the letter, and it is described only here. The primary textual allusion for this paragraph is to Locke's *The Second Treatise of Government*, "Of Political or Civil Society," ch. 7. It is striking that the noble writer alludes to Locke's description of the first artificial society in his single and brief description of natural society. He may be following Bolingbroke's correction of Locke. See *Philosophical Works*, 4:41–53; 107–109. On the other hand, allusions to Lucretius' *De rerum natura* (Bk. 5, lines 783–863, 935–950), and Rousseau's *Discourse on the Origin and Foundations of Inequality Among Men* (*The First and Second Discourses*, pp. 105, 115), suggest that the noble writer is following Rousseau's use of Lucretius and correction of both Locke and Bolingbroke.

[9]This is Locke's expression. Compare n. 8.

owe an implicit Reverence to all the Institutions of our Ancestors, we shall consider these Institutions with all that Modesty with which we ought to conduct ourselves in examining a received Opinion; but with all that Freedom and Candour which we owe to Truth wherever we find it, or however it may contradict our own Notions, or oppose our own Interests. There is a most absurd and audacious Method of reasoning avowed by some Bigots and Enthusiasts, and through Fear assented to by some wiser and better Men; it is this. They argue against a fair Discussion of popular Prejudices, because, say they, tho' they would be found without any reasonable Support, yet the Discovery might be productive of the most dangerous Consequences. Absurd and blasphemous Notion! As if all Happiness was not connected with the Practice of Virtue, which necessarily depends upon the Knowledge of Truth; that is, upon the Knowledge of those unalterable Relations which Providence has ordained that every thing should bear to every other.[10] These Relations, which are Truth itself, the Foundation of Virtue, and consequently, the only Measures of Happiness, should be likewise the only Measures by which we should direct our Reasoning. To these we should conform in good Earnest; and

---

[10]Compare Montesquieu, *The Spirit of the Laws*, Bk. 1, ch. 1.

not think to force Nature, and the whole Order of her System, by a Compliance with our Pride, and Folly, to conform to our artificial Regulations. It is by a Conformity to this Method we owe the Discovery of the few Truths we know, and the little Liberty and rational Happiness we enjoy. We have something fairer Play than a Reasoner could have expected formerly; and we derive Advantages from it which are very visible.

The Fabrick of Superstition has in this our Age and Nation received much ruder Shocks than it had ever felt before; and through the Chinks and Breaches of our Prison, we see such Glimmerings of Light, and feel such refreshing Airs of Liberty, as daily raise our Ardor for more. The Miseries derived to Mankind from Superstition, under the Name of Religion, and of ecclesiastical Tyranny under the Name of Church Government, have been clearly and usefully exposed. We begin to think and to act from Reason and from Nature alone. This is true of several, but still is by far the Majority in the same old State of Blindness and Slavery; and much is it to be feared that we shall perpetually relapse, whilst the real productive Cause of all this superstitious Folly, enthusiastical Nonsense, and holy Tyranny, holds a reverend Place in the Estimation even of those who are otherwise enlightened.

Civil Government borrows a Strength from

ecclesiastical; and artificial Laws receive a Sanc-
tion from artificial Revelations. The Ideas of Religion and Government are closely connected; and
whilst we receive Government as a thing necessary, or even useful to our Well-being, we shall in
spite of us draw in, as a necessary, tho' undesir-
able Consequence, an artificial Religion of some
kind or other. To this the Vulgar will always be
voluntary Slaves; and even those of a Rank of
Understanding superior, will now and then in-
voluntarily feel its Influence. It is therefore of the
deepest Concernment to us to be set right in this
Point; and to be well satisfied whether civil Government be such a Protector from natural Evils,
and such a Nurse and Increaser of Blessings, as
those of warm Imaginations promise. In such a
Discussion, far am I from proposing in the least to
reflect on our most wise Form of Government; no
more than I would in the freer Parts of my
philosophical Writings, mean to object to the Piety, Truth, and Perfection of our most excellent
Church. Both I am sensible have their Foundations on a Rock. No Discovery of Truth can prejudice them. On the contrary, the more closely the
Origin of Religion and Government are examined, the more clearly their Excellencies must appear. They come purified from the Fire. My Business is not with them. Having entered a Protest

against all Objections from these Quarters, I may the more freely enquire from History and Experience, how far Policy has contributed in all Times to alleviate those Evils which Providence, that perhaps has designed us for a State of Imperfection, has imposed; how far our physical Skill has cured our constitutional Disorders; and whether, it may not have introduced new ones, cureable perhaps by no Skill.

In looking over any State to form a Judgment on it; it presents itself in two Lights, the external and the internal. The first, that Relation which it bears in point of Friendship or Enmity to other States. The second, that Relation its component Parts, the Governing, and the Governed, bear to each other. The first Part of the external View of all States, their Relation as Friends, makes so trifling a Figure in History, that I am very sorry to say, it affords me but little Matter on which to expatiate. The good Offices done by one Nation to its Neighbour;* the Support given in publick Distress; the Relief afforded in general Calamity; the

Had his Lordship lived to our Days, to have seen the noble Relief given by this Nation to the distressed Portuguese, *he had perhaps owned this Part of his Argument a little weakened, but we do not think ourselves intitled to alter his Lordship's Words, but that we are bound to follow him exactly.* [11]

[11]The editor may be referring to the earthquake of 1755 which destroyed Lisbon.

Protection granted in emergent Danger; the mutual Return of Kindness and Civility, would afford a very ample and very pleasing Subject for History. But, alas! all the History of all Times, concerning all Nations, does not afford Matter enough to fill ten Pages, though it should be spun out by the Wire-drawing Amplification of a *Guicciardini* himself.[12] The glaring Side is that of Enmity. War is the Matter which fills all History, and consequently the only, or almost the only View in which we can see the External of political Society, is in a hostile Shape; and the only Actions, to which we have always seen, and still see all of them intent, are such, as tend to the Destruction of one another. War, says *Machiavelli*,[13] ought to be the only Study of a Prince; and by a Prince, he means every sort of State however constituted. He ought, says this great political

---

[12]Francesco Guicciardini (1483–1540) was an Italian statesman and historian. He may have been Machiavelli's first influential disciple, although there is some question about the extent to which Guicciardini embraced his friend's political philosophy. See the note below.

[13]Niccolo Machiavelli (1469–1527) was an Italian statesman and philosopher who broke with the ancient philosophical tradition established by Socrates, Plato, and Aristotle. Machiavelli's major works are *Discourses on the First Ten Books of Titus Livius* and *The Prince* whose chapter 14 is referred to here. The noble writer focuses upon the fundamental political issue separating the ancients and moderns. The ancients emphasized internal relations and regarded foreign or external relations, with their inevitable wars, as necessary evils. Machiavelli evaluated politics primarily from the views of external relations and war. For him, internal relations are only a variety of war or external relations.

Doctor, to consider Peace only as a Breathing-time,[a] which gives him Leisure to contrive, and furnishes Ability to execute military Plans. A Meditation on the Conduct of political Societies made old *Hobbes*[14] imagine, that War was the State of Nature; and truly, if a Man judged of the Individuals of our Race by their Conduct when united and packed into Nations and Kingdoms, he might imagine that every sort of Virtue was unnatural and foreign to the Mind of Man.

The first Accounts we have of Mankind are but so many Accounts of their Butcheries.[b] All Empires have been cemented in Blood; and in those early Periods when the Race of Mankind began first to form themselves into Parties and Combinations, the first Effect of the Combination, and indeed the End for which it seems purposely formed, and best calculated, is their mutual Destruction. All ancient History is dark and uncer-

---

[14]Thomas Hobbes (1588–1679) was an English philosopher whose most renowned work is the *Leviathan*. He was the first modern to develop the doctrine of the state of nature and to distinguish that state from the civil state. Adapting Machiavelli, Hobbes claimed that the state of nature is the war of all against all. See *Leviathan*, ch. 13. The noble writer criticizes Hobbes in words very similar to those that Rousseau employed against all philosophers, who, previous to Rousseau, imitated Hobbes and tried to return to the state of nature. Rousseau says the following: "The philosophers who examined the foundations of society have all felt the necessity of going back to the state of nature, but none of them has reached it . . . they spoke about savage man and they described civil man." *The First and Second Discourses*, p. 102.

tain. One thing however is clear. There were Conquerors, and Conquests, in those Days; and consequently, all that Devastation, by which they are formed, and all that Oppression by which they are maintained. We know little of *Sesostris*, [15] but that he led out of *Egypt* an Army of above 700,000 Men; that he over-ran the *Mediterranean* Coast as far as *Colchis;* that in some Places, he met but little Resistance, and of course shed not a great deal of Blood; but that he found in others, a People who knew the Value of their Liberties, and sold them dear. Whoever considers the Army this Conqueror headed, the Space he traversed, and the Opposition he frequently met; with the natural Accidents of Sickness, and the Dearth and Badness of Provision to which he must have been subject[a] in the Variety of Climates and Countries his March lay through, if he knows any thing, he must know, that even the Conqueror's Army

---

[15]Sesostris is the name of several Egyptian kings. According to the Roman historian, Justin, from whom the noble writer takes these incidents, Sesostris I (d. 1926 B.C.) led his army throughout Asia to force its peoples to recognize the pre-eminence of Egypt through some kind of tribute. When he came to invade the land of the Scythians, they resisted, and he fled, abandoning his army. The Scythians then successfully undertook Sesostris's enterprise. The calculation of the war dead are not Justin's. Compare John S. Watson, ed., *Justin, Cornelius, Nepos, and Eutropius* (London: George Bell & Son, 1890), p. 2. Many of the variants from the first edition indicate that the statistics on the war dead are Burke's invention, and he changed them as he wished.

must have suffered greatly; and that, of this immense Number, but a very small Part could have
returned to enjoy the Plunder accumulated by the
Loss of so many of their Companions, and the
Devastation of so considerable a Part of the
World.[a] Considering, I say, the vast Army headed
by this Conqueror, whose unwieldy Weight was
almost alone sufficient to wear down its Strength,
it will be far from Excess to suppose that one half
was lost in the Expedition. If this was the State of
the Victorious, and from the Circumstances, it
must have been this at the least, the Vanquished[b]
must have had a much heavier Loss, as the
greatest Slaughter is always in the Flight, and
great Carnage did in those Times and Countries
ever attend the first Rage of Conquest.[c] It will
therefore be very reasonable to allow on their account as much as, added to the Losses of the
Conqueror, may amount to a Million of Deaths,
and then we shall see this Conqueror, the oldest
we have on the Records of History, (though, as
we have observed before, the Chronology of these
remote Times is extremely uncertain) opening[d] the
Scene by a Destruction of at least one Million[e] of
his Species, unprovoked but by his Ambition,
without any Motives but Pride, Cruelty, and
Madness, and without any Benefit to himself; (for

Justin[16] expressly tells us, he did not maintain his Conquests) but solely to make so many People, in so distant Countries, feel experimentally, how severe a Scourge Providence intends for the human Race, when he gives one Man the Power over many, and arms his naturally impotent, and feeble Rage, with the Hands of Millions, who know no common Principle of Action, but a blind Obedience to the Passions of their Ruler.

The next Personage who figures in the Tragedies of this ancient Theatre is *Semiramis:*[17] For we have no Particulars of *Ninus,* but that he made immense and rapid Conquests, which doubtless were not compassed without the usual Carnage. We see an Army of above three Millions employed by this martial Queen in a War against the *Indians.* We see the *Indians* arming a yet

---

[16]See n. 15.

[17]Semiramis was the wife of Ninus, a king of Assyria. He is not the unknown that the noble writer claims he is. In fact, Justin opens his history with Ninus because he invented the empire, that is, a political unit comprised largely of conquered peoples. In Justin, monarchy begins in consent, and Ninus perverted it. Sesostris and the Scythians did not make territorial conquests. Here is a fundamental dispute about the founding of monarchies and perhaps of civil society altogether. In contrast to Justin and Locke, who refers to Justin in this regard (see *The Second Treatise of Government,* sect. 103), the noble writer maintains that civil society's original purpose is use for conquest.

Semiramis, in her own right, might be considered the first usurper. She posed as her son, the true heir, upon the death of Ninus. Although her Indian campaign was repulsed, she was otherwise a successful conqueror. Boccaccio asserts that she had an incestuous relationship with her son and that, out of shame, he killed her. See Giovanni Boccaccio, *De claris mulieribus,* ch. 4.

greater; and we behold a War continued with much Fury, and with various Success. This ends in the Retreat of the Queen,[a] with scarce a third of the Troops employed in the Expedition; an Expedition, which at this rate must have cost two Millions of Souls on her part; and it is not unreasonable to judge that the Country which was the Seat of War, must have been an equal Sufferer. But I am content to detract from this, and to suppose that the *Indians* lost only half so much, and then the Account stands thus:[b] In this War alone, (for *Semiramis*[c] had other Wars) in this single Reign, and in this one Spot of the Globe, did three Millions[d] of Souls expire, with all the horrid and shocking Circumstances which attend all Wars, and in a Quarrel, in which none of the Sufferers could have the least rational Concern.

The *Babylonian, Assyrian, Median,* and *Persian*[18] Monarchies must have poured out Seas of Blood in their Formation, and in their Destruction. The Armies and Fleets of *Xerxes,* their Numbers, the glorious Stand made against them, and the unfor-

---

[18]This history proceeds geographically from east to west rather than chronologically. It is a record of the bloody spread of western civilization. The noble writer uses no dates in the letter whatsoever. He indicates the relation between events by phrases like "about this time" (compare p. 34) which are not always accurate. He may be following Montesquieu's practice in *Considerations on the Causes of the Greatness of Romans and their Decline* of refusing to use the Christian convention, of dating events from the birth of Christ, by not mentioning any dates at all.

tunate Event of all his mighty Preparations, are known to every body. In this Expedition, draining[a] half *Asia* of its Inhabitants, he led an Army of about two Millions to be slaughtered, and wasted, by a thousand fatal Accidents, in the same Place where his Predecessors had before by a similar Madness consumed the Flower of so many Kingdoms, and wasted the Force of so extensive an Empire. It is a cheap Calculation to say, that the *Persian* Empire in its Wars, against the *Greeks*, and *Sythians*, threw away at least four Millions of its[b] Subjects, to say nothing of its[c] other Wars, and the Losses sustained in them. These were their Losses abroad; but the War was brought home to them, first by *Agesilaus*, and afterwards, by *Alexander*.[19] I have not, in this Retreat, the Books necessary to make very exact Calculations; nor is it necessary to give more than Hints to one of your Lordship's Erudition. You will recollect his uninterrupted Series of Success. You will run over his Battles. You will call to mind the Carnage which was made. You will give a Glance of the Whole, and you will agree with me; that to form this Hero no less than twelve

---

[19]Xerxes was the Persian king who led the second great Persian invasion of Greece, which was defeated at the battle of Salamis (480 B.C.). Agesilaus was a Spartan king who invaded Asia Minor without permanent success (396 B.C.). Alexander, of course, was Alexander the Great (356–323), the Macedonian king who conquered Persia and constructed a Hellenic empire stretching from Greece to Persia to Egypt.

hundred thousand Lives must have been sac-
rificed; but no sooner had he fallen himself a Sacrifice to his Vices, than a thousand Breaches were
made for Ruin to enter, and give the last hand to
this Scene of Misery and Destruction. His King-
dom was rent and divided; which served to employ the more distinct Parts to tear each other to
Pieces, and bury the whole in Blood and Slaughter. The kings of *Syria* and of *Egypt,* the Kings of
Pergamus and *Macedon,* without Intermission wor-
ried each other for above two hundred Years; until
at last a strong Power arising in the West, rushed
in upon them and silenced their Tumults, by in-
volving all the contending Parties in the same Destruction. It is little to say, that the Contentions
between the Successors of *Alexander* depopulated
that Part of the World of at least two Millions.[a]

The Struggle between the *Macedonians* and
Greeks, and before that, the Disputes of the *Greek*
Commonwealths among themselves, for an un-
profitable Superiority, form one of the bloodiest
Scenes in History. One is astonished how such a
small Spot could furnish Men sufficient to sacrifice to the pitiful Ambition of possessing five or
six thousand more Acres, or two or three more
Villages: Yet to see the Acrimony and Bitterness
with which this was disputed between the *Athenians* and *Lacedemonians;* what Armies cut off;

what Fleets sunk, and burnt; what a Number of Cities sacked, and their Inhabitants slaughtered, and captived; one would be induced to believe the Decision of the Fate of Mankind at least, depended upon it! But these Disputes ended as all such ever have done, and ever will do; in a real Weakness of all Parties; a momentary Shadow, and Dream of Power in some one; and the Subjection of all to the Yoke of a Stranger, who knows how to profit of their Divisions. This at least was the case of the *Greeks;* and sure, from the earliest Accounts of them, to their Absorption into the *Roman* Empire, we cannot judge that their intestine Divisions, and[a] their foreign Wars, consumed less than three Millions of their Inhabitants.

What an *Aceldama,*[20] what a Field of Blood *Sicily* has been in ancient times, whilst the Mode of its Government was controverted between the republican and tyrannical Parties, and the Possession struggled for by the Natives, the *Greeks,* the *Carthaginians,* and the *Romans,* your Lordship will easily recollect. You will remember the total Destruction of such Bodies as an Army of 300,000 Men. You will find every Page of its History dyed in Blood, and blotted and confounded by

---

[20]Aceldema means "field of blood" and is the name given to the potter's field, where Judas hanged himself, which subsequently was purchased by the priests with the thirty pieces of silver that he earned for betraying Jesus, and which was thereafter used for burying strangers.

Tumults, Rebellions, Massacres, Assassinations, Proscriptions, and a Series of Horror beyond the Histories perhaps of any other Nation in the World; though the Histories of all Nations are made up of similar Matter. I once more excuse myself in point of Exactness for want of Books. But I shall estimate the Slaughters in this Island but at two Millions; which your Lordship will find much short of the Reality.

Let us pass by the Wars, and the Consequences of them, which wasted *Grecia-Magna*, before the *Roman* Power prevailed in that Part of *Italy*. They are perhaps exaggerated; therefore I shall only rate them at one Million. Let us hasten to open that great Scene which establishes the *Roman* Empire, and forms the grand Catastrophe of the ancient Drama. This Empire, whilst in its Infancy, began by an Effusion of human Blood scarcely credible. The neighbouring little States teemed for new Destruction: The *Sabines*, the *Samnites*, the *Æqui*, the *Volsci*, the *Hetrurians*, were broken by a Series of Slaughters which had no Interruption, for some hundreds of Years; Slaughters which upon all sides consumed more than two Millions of the wretched People. The *Gauls* rushing into *Italy* about this Time, added the total Destruction of their own Armies to those of the ancient Inhabitants. In short, it were hardly possible to con-

ceive a more horrid and bloody Picture, if that
which the *Punic* Wars that ensued soon after did
not present one, that far exceeds it. Here we find
that Climax of Devastation, and Ruin, which
seemed to shake the whole Earth. The Extent of
this War which vexed[a] so many Nations, and both
Elements, and the Havock of the human Species
caused in both, really astonishes beyond Expression, when it is nakedly considered, and those
Matters which are apt to divert our Attention
from it, the Characters, Actions, and Designs of
the Persons concerned, are not taken into the Account. These Wars, I mean those called the *Punic*
Wars, could not have stood the human Race in
less than three[b] Millions of the Species. And yet
this forms but a Part only, and a very small Part,
of the Havock caused by the *Roman* Ambition.
The War with *Mithridates*[21,c] was very little less
bloody; that Prince cut off at one Stroke 150,000
Romans by a Massacre. In that War *Sylla*[22] de-

---

[21]Mithridates VI (c.131–63) was the king of Pontus, a country in
northeast Asia Minor on the Black Sea. He engaged the Romans in three
wars. After the third, he was soundly defeated and had a slave kill him.

[22]Sylla or Lucius Cornelius Sulla (138–78) was a Roman general
known for his cruelty. He was responsible for the sack of Athens.
Named dictator, he tried to return the Roman constitution to its earlier,
more aristocratic form. In order to achieve this reformation, he employed
proscription, the publishing of lists of persons condemned to death with
their properties confiscated.

stroyed 300,000 Men at *Cheronea*. He[a] defeated
Mithridates' Army under *Dorilaus*, and slew
300,000. This great and unfortunate Prince[b] lost
another 300,000 before *Cyzicum*. In the course of
the War he had innumerable other Losses; and
having many Intervals of Success, he revenged
them severely. He was at last totally overthrown;
and he crushed to Pieces the King of *Armenia* his
Ally by the Greatness of his Ruin. All who had
Connexions with him shared the same Fate. The
merciless Genius of *Sylla* had its full Scope; and
the Streets of *Athens* were not the only ones
which ran with Blood. At this Period, the Sword,
glutted with foreign Slaughter, turned its Edge
upon the Bowels of the *Roman* Republick itself;
and presented a Scene of Cruelties and Treasons
enough almost to obliterate the Memory of all the
external Devastations. I intended, my Lord, to
have proceeded in a sort of Method in estimating
the Numbers of Mankind cut off in these Wars
which we have on Record. But I am obliged to
alter my Design. Such a tragical Uniformity of
Havock and Murder would disgust your Lordship
as much as it would me; and I confess I already
feel my Eyes ake by keeping them so long intent
on so bloody a Prospect. I shall observe little on
the *Servile,* the *Social,* the *Gallic,* and *Spanish*

Wars;[23] not upon those with *Jugurtha,* nor *Antiochus,*[24] nor many others equally important, and carried on with equal Fury. The Butcheries of *Julius Cæsar* alone, are calculated by some body else; the Numbers he has been a means of destroying have been reckoned at 1,200,000. But to give your Lordship an Idea that may serve as a Standard, by which to measure, in some degree, the others; you will turn your Eyes on *Judea;* a very inconsiderable Spot of the Earth in itself, though ennobled by the singular Events which had their Rise in that Country.

This Spot happened, it matters not here by what means, to become at several times extremely populous, and to supply Men for Slaughters scarcely credible, if other well-known and well-attested ones had not given them a Colour. The first settling of the *Jews* here, was attended by an almost entire Extirpation of all the former Inhabi-

---

[23]A series of Roman wars in Europe roughly from 134 until 51. The servile wars were slave uprisings, the most famous of which was led by Spartacus and succeeded in capturing, for a short period, southern Italy. The social war was a revolt by the Roman allies to gain recognition as Roman citizens. The Spanish and Gallic wars consolidated the Roman rule in Spain and Gaul. The wealth and power, which Julius Caesar gained as general in the Gallic wars, allowed him to make his bid to become the master of Rome.

[24]Jugurtha (c. 156–104) was king of Numidia. In securing his throne, he killed some Italians and provided the Romans with an excuse for invasion. They captured Numidia and brought Jugurtha to Rome where he was executed. Antiochus (d. 187 B. C.) was a king of Syria. He challenged the Roman expansion into Greece but was forced to give up all Syrian territory on the sea.

tants. Their own civil Wars, and those with their petty Neighbours, consumed vast Multitudes almost every Year for several Centuries;[25] and the Irruptions of the Kings of *Babylon* and *Assyria* made immense Ravages.[26] Yet we have their History but partially, in an indistinct confused manner; so that I shall only throw the strong Point of Light upon that Part which coincides with *Roman* History,[27] and of that Part only on the Point of Time when they received the great and final Stroke which made them no more a Nation; a Stroke which is allowed to have cut off little less than two Millions of that People. I say nothing of the Loppings made from that Stock whilst it stood; nor from the Suckers that grew out of the old Root ever since. But if in this inconsiderable Part of the Globe, such a Carnage has been made in two or three short Reigns and that this Carnage, great as it is, makes but a minute Part of what the Histories of that People inform us they suffered; what shall we judge of Countries more extended, and which have waged Wars by far more considerable?

Instances of this Sort compose the Uniform of History. But there have been Periods when no less

---

[25]Compare Joshua and Judges.
[26]Compare 2 Kings 24–25, and Jeremiah 52.
[27]Compare Flavius Josephus, *The Wars of the Jews*.

than universal Destruction to the Race of Mankind seems to have been threatened. When the *Goths*, the *Vandals*, and the *Huns*[28] poured into *Gaul, Italy, Spain, Greece*, and *Africa*, carrying Destruction before them as they advanced, and leaving horrid Desarts every where behind them. *Vastum ubique silentium, secreti colles; fumantia procul tecta; nemo exploratoribus obvius*, is what *Tacitus* calls *facies Victoriæ*.[29] It is always so; but was here emphatically so. From the North proceeded the Swarms of *Goths, Vandals, Huns, Ostrogoths*, who ran towards the South into *Africa* itself, which suffered as all to the North had done. About this Time, another Torrent of Barbarians, animated by the same Fury, and encouraged by the same Success, poured out of the South, and ravaged all to the North-east and West, to the remotest Parts of *Persia* on one hand, and to the Banks of the *Loire* or further on the other; destroying all the proud and curious Monuments of human Art, that not

---

[28]The Vandals and Goths (Visigoths and Ostrogoths) were Germanic peoples, and the Huns a people of unknown origin, who invaded the Roman Empire in the fourth, fifth, and sixth centuries and caused its collapse.

[29]"Everywhere a vast silence, lonely hills; smoking roofs, no one is met by the scouts" is what Tacitus calls "the face of victory." *Agricola*, 38 (trans. J. Brian Benestad). This passage describes the Roman conquest of Britain in the first century A.D. The first effect of the passage in context is to suggest that there was no difference between the wars that destroyed the empire and those which created it. Implicitly it raises the question of whether conquests of uncivilized peoples by more civilized peoples are not more justified than the reverse.

even the Memory might seem to survive of the former Inhabitants.[30] What has been done since, and what will continue to be done whilst the same Inducements to War continue, I shall not dwell upon. I shall only in one Word mention the horrid Effects of Bigotry and Avarice, in the Conquest of *Spanish America*; a Conquest on a low Estimation effected by the Murder of ten Millions of the Species.[31] I shall draw to a Conclusion of this Part, by making a general Calculation of the Whole. I think I have actually mentioned above thirty-six Millions.[a] I have not particularized any more. I don't pretend to Exactness; therefore for the sake of a general View, I shall lay together all those actually slain in Battles, or who have perished in a no less miserable manner by the other destructive Consequences of War from the Beginning of the World[b] to this Day, in the four Parts of it, at[c] a thousand times as much;[32] no

---

[30]These were the Islamic invasions which spread from Arabia in the sixth century but did not reach Europe until the eighth century. Their farthest penetration was Tours, France, where the Moors were defeated in 732. The noble writer points out the viciousness of the wars but not the reason for it. The wars were religiously motivated.

[31]The noble writer cuts off his review of war just before the Protestant Reformation. By mentioning the Spanish, he alludes to his reason: he does not wish to speak about the religious wars between Christians, especially those wars most familiar to the British. For all of his attack on artificial religion, he gives up his chase exactly when religious abuses are the most obvious. In a backhanded manner, he protects religion.

[32]The noble writer's method of determining the total killed by war and society (multiplying his own particularized total of 36 million by one

exaggerated[a] Calculation, allowing for Time and Extent. We have not perhaps spoke of the five-hundredth Part; I am sure I have not of what is actually ascertained in History; but how much of these Butcheries are only expressed in Generals, what Part of Time History has never reached, and what vast Spaces of the habitable Globe it has not embraced, I need not mention to your Lordship. I need not enlarge on these Torrents of silent and inglorious Blood which have glutted the thirsty Sands of *Africa*, or discoloured the polar Snow, or fed the savage Forests of *America* for so many Ages of continual War; shall I, to justify my Calculations from the Charge of Extravagance, add to the Account those Skirmishes which happen in all Wars, without being singly of sufficient Dignity in Mischief, to merit a Place in History, but which by their Frequency compensate for this comparative

---

thousand to arrive at an estimate of 36 billion killed by society) has been used as major evidence to support that position that the *Vindication* is entirely satirical. See J.C. Weston, Jr., "The Ironic Purpose of Burke's *Vindication* Vindicated," *Journal of the History of Ideas*, 19 (June 1958): 435–441. Burke in the preface draws our attention to the calculations made in the letter (p. 10), and one of his major revisions in the second edition was to alter the particularized death count. Ultimately, these figures blame all human deaths (later, the noble writer modifies it to almost all) on civil society. We can see this by dividing 4000 years, the age at which, probably satirically, the earth is put, by seventy (since seventy times the number alive today have been killed by war). The result is 57 years, approximately the lifetime of a generation. Behind these calculations is the claim that when man becomes conscious of death, he becomes civil man.

Innocence; shall I inflame the Account by those general Massacres which have devoured whole Cities and Nations; those wasting Pestilences, those consuming Famines, and all those Furies that follow in the Train of War?[a] I have no need to exaggerate; and I have purposely avoided a Parade of Eloquence on this Occasion. I should despise it upon any Occasion; else in mentioning these Slaughters, it is obvious how much the whole might be heightened, by an affecting Description of the Horrors that attend the wasting of Kingdoms, and sacking of Cities. But I do not write to the Vulgar, nor to that which only governs the Vulgar, their Passions. I go upon a naked and moderate Calculation, just enough, without a pedantical Exactness, to give your Lordship some Feeling of the Effects of political Society. I charge the whole of these Effects on political Society. I avow the Charge, and I shall presently make it good to your Lordship's Satisfaction. The Numbers I particularized are about thirty-six Millions. Besides those killed in Battles I have something, not half what the Matter would have justified, but something I have said, concerning the Consequences of War even more dreadful than that monstrous Carnage itself which shocks our Humanity, and almost staggers our Belief. So that allowing me in my Exuberance one way, for my

Deficiencies in the other, you will find me not un-reasonable.[a] I think the Numbers of Men now upon Earth are computed at 500 Millions at the most. Here the Slaughter of Mankind, on what you will call a small Calculation, amounts to up-wards of seventy times[b] the Number of Souls this Day on the Globe. A Point which may furnish matter of Reflection to one less inclined to draw Consequences than your Lordship.

I now come to shew, that Political Society is justly chargeable with much the greatest Part of this Destruction of the Species. To give[c] the fairest Play to every side of the Question, I will own that there is a Haughtiness, and Fierceness in human Nature, which will cause innumerable Broils, place Men in what Situation you please; but own-ing this, I still insist in charging it[d] to political Regulations, that these Broils are so frequent, so cruel, and attended with Consequences so de-plorable.[e] In a State of Nature, it had been im-possible to find a Number of Men, sufficient for such Slaughters, agreed in the same bloody Pur-pose; or allowing that they might have come to such an Agreement,[f] (an impossible Supposition) yet the Means that simple Nature has supplied them with, are by no means adequate to such an End;[g] many Scratches, many Bruises undoubtedly would be received upon all hands; but only a few, a very few Deaths. Society, and Politicks, which have given us these destructive Views, have given us also[a] the Means of satisfying them. From the earliest Dawnings of Policy to this Day, the Invention of Men has been sharpening and improving the Mystery of Murder, from the first rude Essays of Clubs and Stones, to the present Perfection of Gunnery, Cannoneering, Bombarding, Mining,[b] and all these Species of artificial, learned, and refined Cruelty, in[c] which we are now so expert, and which make a principal Part of what Politicians have taught us to believe is our principal Glory.[33]

How far mere Nature would have carried us, we may judge by the Examples of those Animals, who still follow her Laws, and even of those[d] to whom she has given Dispositions more fierce, and Arms more terrible than ever she intended we should use. It is an incontestable Truth, that there is more Havock made in one Year by Men, of Men, than has been made by all the Lions, Tygers, Panthers, Ounces, Leopards, Hyenas, Rhinoceroses, Elephants, Bears, and Wolves, upon their several Species, since the Beginning of the World; though these agree ill enough with each other, and have a much greater Proportion of

---

[33]Compare Montesquieu, *The Persian Letters,* letters 105 and 106.

Rage and Fury in their Composition than we have. But with respect to you, ye Legislators, ye Civilizers of Mankind! ye *Orpheuses, Moseses, Minoses, Solons, Theseuses, Lycurguses, Numas!*[34] with Respect to you be it spoken, your Regulations have done more Mischief in cold Blood, than all the Rage of the fiercest Animals in their greatest Terrors, or Furies, have ever done, or ever could do!

These Evils are not accidental. Whoever will take the pains to consider the Nature of Society, will find they result directly from its Constitution. For as *Subordination,* or in other Words, the Reciprocation of Tyranny, and Slavery, is requisite to support these Societies, the Interest, the Ambition, the Malice, or the Revenge, nay even the Whim and Caprice of one ruling Man among them, is enough to arm all the rest, without any private Views of their own, to the worst and blackest Purposes; and what is at once lamentable

---

[34]Each is an ancient lawgiver. Orpheus is a mystical figure who supposedly established the Greek orphic rites and their accompanying code. Moses is the lawgiver of Israel, Minos of Crete, Solon of democratic Athens, Theseus the founder of Athens, Lycurgus the lawgiver of Sparta, and Numa of Rome. The obvious contrast is with Machiavelli. See *The Prince,* ch. 6; and the *Discourses,* Bk. 1, ch. 1; Bk. 3, chs. 10 and 11. He stresses that the founders formed cities by good arms, that is, by force, and not by good laws. The noble writer blames the lawgivers and hence implies that they are more responsible for the formation of nations than the armed founders. His list also is weighted toward men who reputedly received their laws from a god or God.

and ridiculous, these Wretches engage under those Banners with a Fury greater than if they were animated by Revenge for their own proper Wrongs.

It is no less worth observing, that this artificial Division of Mankind, into separate Societies, is a perpetual Source in itself of Hatred and Dissention among them. The Names which distinguish them are enough to blow up Hatred, and Rage. Examine History; consult present Experience; and you will find, that far the greater Part of the Quarrels between several Nations, had scarce any other Occasion, than that these Nations were different Combinations of People, and called by different Names;[a]—to an *Englishman*, the Name of a *Frenchman*, a *Spaniard*, an *Italian*, much more a *Turk*, or a *Tartar*, raise of course Ideas of Hatred, and Contempt. If you would inspire this Compatriot of ours with Pity or Regard, for one of these; would you not hide that Distinction?[b] You would not pray him to compassionate the poor *Frenchman*, or the unhappy *German*. Far from it; you would speak of him as a *Foreigner*, an Accident to which all are liable. You would represent him as a *Man:* one partaking with us of the same common Nature, and subject to the same Law. There is something so averse from[c] our Nature in these artificial political Distinctions, that we need no other

Trumpet to kindle us to War, and Destruction. But there is something so benign and healing in the general Voice of Humanity, that maugre all our Regulations to prevent it, the simple Name of Man[a] applied properly, never fails to work a salutary Effect.

This natural unpremediated Effect of Policy on the unpossessed Passions of Mankind, appears on other Occasions. The very Name of a Politician, a Statesman, is sure to cause Terror and Hatred; it has always connected with it the Ideas of Treachery, Cruelty, Fraud and Tyranny; and those Writers who have faithfully unveiled the Mysteries of State-freemasonry, have ever been held in general Detestation, for even knowing so perfectly a Theory so detestable. The Case of *Machiavelli* seems at first sight something hard in that Respect. He is obliged to bear the Iniquities of those whose Maxims and Rules of Government he published. His Speculation is more abhorred than their Practice.

But if there were no other Arguments against artificial Society than this I am going to mention, methinks it ought to fall by this[b] one only. All Writers on the Science of Policy are agreed, and they agree with Experience, that all Governments must frequently infringe the Rules of Justice to support themselves; that Truth must give way to

Dissimulation; Honesty to Convenience; and Humanity itself to the reigning Interest.[35] The Whole of this Mystery of Iniquity is called the Reason of State. It is a Reason, which I own I cannot penetrate. What Sort of a Protection is this of the general Right, that is maintained by infringing the Rights of Particulars? What sort of Justice is this, which is inforced by Breaches of its own Laws? These Paradoxes I leave to be solved by the able heads of Legislators and Politicians. For my part, I say[a] what a plain Man would say on such an Occasion. I can never believe, that any Institution agreeable to Nature, and proper for Mankind, could find it necessary, or even expedient in any Case whatsoever to do, what the best and worthiest Instincts of Mankind warn us to avoid. But no wonder, that what is set up in Opposition to the State of Nature, should preserve itself by trampling upon the Law of Nature.

To prove, that these Sort of policed Societies are

---

[35]This is a paraphrase of Machiavelli, *Discourses*, Bk. 1, ch. 3. "All those who have written upon civil institutions demonstrate (and history is full of examples to support them) that whoever desires to found a state and give it laws, must start with assuming that all men are bad and ever ready to display their vicious nature, whenever they may find occasion for it." *The Prince and the Discourses,* trans. Christian E. Detmold, The Modern Library (New York: Random House, 1950), p. 117.

There are differences between the noble writer's and Machiavelli's perspectives. The former accepts Machiavelli's observation as accurate—legislators must assume all men are wicked—but he claims that this assumption, although necessary, is false and therefore unjust. There are good men, but laws are not made for them.

43

a Violation offered to Nature, and a Constraint upon the human Mind, it needs only to look upon the sanguinary Measures, and Instruments of Violence which are every where used to support them. Let us take a Review of the Dungeons, Whips, Chains, Racks, Gibbets, with which every Society is abundantly stored, by which hundreds of Victims are annually offered up to support a dozen or two in Pride and Madness, and Millions in an abject Servitude, and Dependence. There was a Time, when I looked with a reverential Awe on these Mysteries of Policy; but Age, Experience, and Philosophy have rent the Veil; and I view this *Sanctum Sanctorum*, at least, without any enthusiastick Admiration. I acknowledge indeed, the Necessity of such a Proceeding in such Institutions; but I must have a very mean Opinion of Institutions[a] where such Proceedings are necessary.

It is a Misfortune, that in no Part of the Globe natural Liberty and natural Religion are to be found pure, and free from the Mixture of political Adulterations. Yet we have implanted in us by Providence Ideas, Axioms, Rules, of what is pious, just, fair, honest, which no political Craft, nor learned Sophistry, can entirely expel from our Breasts. By these we judge, and we cannot otherwise judge of the several artificial Modes of

Religion and Society, and determine of them as they approach to, or recede from this Standard.

The simplest form of Government is *Despotism*, where all the inferior Orbs of Power are moved merely by the Will of the Supreme, and all that are subjected to them, directed in the same Manner, merely by the occasional Will of the Magistrate. This Form, as it is the most simple, so it is infinitely the most general. Scarce any Part of the World is exempted from its Power. And in those few Places where Men enjoy what they call Liberty, it is continually in a tottering Situation, and makes greater and greater Strides to that Gulph of Despotism which at last swallows up every Species of Government. This Manner of ruling being directed merely by the Will of the weakest, and generally the worst Man in the Society, becomes the most foolish and capricious Thing, at the same time that it is the most terrible and destructive that well can be conceived. In a Despotism the principal Person finds, that let the Want, Misery, and Indigence of his Subjects, be what they will, he can yet possess abundantly of every thing to gratify his most insatiable Wishes. He does more. He finds that these Gratifications increase in proportion to the Wretchedness and Slavery of his Subjects. Thus encouraged both by Passion and Interest to trample on the publick Welfare,[a]

and by his Station placed above both Shame and
Fear, he proceeds to the most horrid and shocking
Outrages upon Mankind. Their Persons become
Victims of his Suspicions. The slightest Displea-
sure is Death; and a disagreeable Aspect is often
as great a Crime as High-treason. In the court of
Nero a Person of Learning, of unquestioned Merit,
and of unsuspected Loyalty, was put to Death for
no other Reason than that he had a pedantick
Countenance which displeased the Emperor.[36]
This very Monster of Mankind appeared in the
Beginning of his Reign to be a Person of Virtue.
Many of the greatest Tyrants on the Records of
History have begun their Reigns[a] in the fairest
Manner. But the Truth is, this unnatural Power
corrupts both the Heart, and the Understanding.
And to prevent the least Hope of Amendment, a
King is ever surrounded by a Crowd of infamous
Flatterers, who find their Account in keeping him
from the least Light of Reason, till all Ideas of Rec-
titude and Justice are utterly erased from his
Mind. When *Alexander* had in his Fury inhumanly
butchered one of his best Friends, and bravest
Captains; on the Return of Reason he began to

---

[36]This may be an allusion to Nero's ordering the suicide of his tutor,
the philosopher and poet, Seneca, for allegedly participating in a plot to
disthrone the emperor. Nero's virtuous early reign may have been a result of Seneca's influence.

conceive an Horror suitable to the Guilt of such a Murder. In this Juncture, his Council came to his Assistance. But what did his Council? They found him out a Philosopher who gave him Comfort. And in what Manner did this Philosopher comfort him for the Loss of such a Man, and heal his Conscience, flagrant with the Smart of such a Crime? You have the Matter at Length in *Plutarch*. He told him; *"that let a Sovereign do what he will, all his actions are just and lawful, because they are his."*[37] The Palaces of all Princes abound with such courtly Philosophers. The Consequence was such

---

[37]This is a reference to the murder of Cleitus by Alexander the Great during one of the king's banquets. After considerable drinking, Alexander joined some singing which mocked the older Macedonians. Cleitus responded by reminding Alexander that he saved the king's life and by criticizing Alexander's disowning of his father Philip and claiming descent from the God Ammon. In a drunken rage, Alexander slew Cleitus. The king lamented the deed for days. Two philosophers were sent for to soothe him: Callisthenes, the nephew of Aristotle, and Anaxarchus. The noble writer neglects to mention Callisthenes who did not justify the murder and who himself ultimately died in prison because he did not adore Alexander in the eastern fashion. Anaxarchus admittedly justified the deed. Still the noble writer, whose apparent purpose is to defend philosophy, distorts the tale to philosophy's disadvantage. He also distorts Anaxarchus' speech. In Plutarch it reads, "Knowest thou not," said he, "That Zeus has Justice and Law seated beside him, in order that everything that is done may be lawful and just?" Bernadotte Perrin, trans., *Plutarch's Lives* (Cambridge, Mass.: Harvard University Press, 1958), 7:376–77. In fact the passage as quoted more resembles a statement in Hobbes's *Leviathan* than Anaxarchus' words. "Fourthly, because every Subject is by this Institution Author of all the Actions, and Judgments of the Soveraigne Instituted; it followes, that whatsoever he doth, it can be no injury to any of his Subjects; nor ought he to be by any of them accused of Injustice." Thomas Hobbes, *Leviathan* (New York: Dutton, 1965), p. 92. Bolingbroke criticized Hobbes for extending Anaxarchus' flatteries of Alexander to all despots. See *Philosophical Works*, 4:17.

as might be expected. He grew every Day a Monster more abandoned to unnatural Lust, to Debauchery, to Drunkenness, and to Murder. And yet this was originally a great Man, of uncommon Capacity, and a strong Propensity to Virtue. But unbounded Power proceeds Step by Step, until it has eradicated every laudable Principle. It has been remarked, that there is no Prince so bad, whose Favourites and Ministers are not worse. There is hardly any Prince without a Favourite, by whom he is governed in as arbitrary a Manner as he governs the Wretches subjected to him. Here the Tyranny is doubled. There are two Courts, and two Interests; both very different from the Interests of the People. The Favourite knows that the Regard of a Tyrant is as unconstant and capricious as that of a Woman; and concluding his Time to be short, he makes haste to fill up the Measure of his Iniquity, in Rapine, in Luxury, and in Revenge. Every Avenue to the Throne is shut up. He oppresses, and ruins the People, whilst he persuades the Prince, that those Murmurs raised by his own Oppression are the Effects of Disaffection to the Prince's Government. Then is the natural Violence of Despotism inflamed, and aggravated by Hatred and Revenge. To deserve well of the State is a Crime against the Prince. To be popular, and to be a Traitor, are considered as

synonimous Terms. Even[a] Virtue is dangerous, as
an aspiring Quality, that claims an Esteem by itself, and independent of the Countenance of the
Court. What has been said of the chief, is true of
the inferior Officers of this Species of Government; each in his Province exercising the same
Tyranny, and grinding the People by an Oppression, the more severely felt, as it is near them,
and exercised by base and subordinate Persons.
For the Gross of the People; they are considered
as a mere Herd of Cattle; and really in a little Time
become no better; all Principle of honest Pride, all
Sense of the Dignity of their Nature, is lost in
their Slavery. The Day, says *Homer*, which makes a
Man a Slave, takes away half his Worth;[38] and in
fact, he loses every Impulse to Action, but that
low and base one of Fear. In this kind of Government human Nature is not only abused and
insulted, but it is actually degraded and sunk into
a Species of Brutality. The Consideration of this
made Mr. Locke say, with great Justice, that a
Government of this kind was worse than Anar-
chy; indeed it is so abhorred, and detested by all
who live under Forms that have a milder Appearance, that there is scarce a rational Man in *Europe*,
that would not prefer Death to *Asiatick* Des-

---

[38]See *Odyssey*, Bk. 17, lines 322–23.

potism. Here then we have the Acknowledgement of a great Philosopher, that an irregular State of Nature is preferable to such a Government;[39] we have the Consent of all sensible and generous Men, who carry it yet further, and avow that Death itself is preferable; and yet this Species of Government, so justly condemned, and so generally detested, is what infinitely the greater Part of Mankind groan under, and have groaned under from the Beginning. So that by sure and uncontested Principles, the greatest Part of the Governments on Earth must be concluded Tyrannies, Impostures, Violations of the Natural Rights of Mankind, and worse than the most disorderly Anarchies. How much other Forms exceed this, we shall consider immediately.

In all Parts of the World, Mankind, however debased, retains still the Sense of *Feeling;* the Weight of Tyranny, at last, becomes insupportable; but the Remedy is not so easy; in general, the only Remedy by which they attempt to cure the Tyranny, is to change the Tyrant. This is, and always was the Case for the greater Part. In some Countries however, were found Men of more

---

[39]John Locke (1632–1704) was an English political philosopher and the classic proponent of liberalism. For Locke's comparison of absolute monarchy (despotism) and the state of nature, see *The Second Treatise of Government,* sect. 13.

Penetration; who discovered, *"that to live by one Man's Will, was the Cause of all Men's Misery."*[40] They therefore changed their former Method, and assembling the Men in their several Societies, the most[a] respectable for their Understanding and Fortunes, they confided to them the Charge of the publick Welfare. This originally formed what is called an *Aristocracy.* They hoped, it would be impossible that such a Number could ever join in any Design against the general Good; and they promised themselves a great deal of Security and Happiness, from the united Counsels of so many able and experienced Persons. But it is now found by abundant Experience, that an *Aristocracy,* and a *Despotism,* differ but in Name; and that a People, who are in general excluded from any Share of the Legislative, are to all Intents and Purposes, as much Slaves, when twenty, independent of them, govern, as when but one domineers. The Tyranny is even more felt, as every Individual of the Nobles has the Haughtiness of a Sultan; the People are more miserable, as they seem on the Verge of Liberty, from which they are for ever debarred,

---

[40]This quotation is nearly an exact reproduction of a line from *Of the Laws of Ecclesiastical Polity* by Richard Hooker (c. 1554–1600), an English theologian and political philosopher. The line in Hooker is, "that to live by one man's will became the cause of all men's misery." Bk. 1, sect. 10. Locke reproduces this line, along with the paragraph to which it belongs, in a footnote to section 94 of *The Second Treatise of Government.*

this fallacious Idea of Liberty,[a] whilst it presents a vain Shadow of Happiness to the Subject, binds faster the Chains of his[b] Subjection. What is left undone, by the natural Avarice and Pride of those who are raised above the others, is compleated by their Suspicions, and their Dread[c] of losing an Authority, which has no Support in the common Utility of the Nation. A *Genoese,* or a *Venetian* Republick, is a concealed *Despotism;* where you find the same Pride of the Rulers, the same base Subjection of the People, the same bloody Maxims of a suspicious Policy. In one respect the *Aristocracy* is worse than the *Despotism.* A Body Politick, whilst it retains its Authority, never changes its Maxims; a *Despotism,* which is this Day horrible to a Supreme Degree, by the Caprice natural to the Heart of Man, may, by the same Caprice otherwise exerted, be as lovely the next; in a Succession, it is possible to meet with some good Princes. If there have been *Tiberiuses, Caligulas, Neros,* there have been likewise the serener Days of *Vespasians, Tituses, Trajans,* and *Antonines;*[41] but a Body Politick is not influenced by Caprice or Whim; it proceeds in a regular Manner; its Succession is insensible; and every Man as he enters

---

[41]All were Roman emperors. The first set were members of Julius Caesar's family. The next six (there were three Antonines) reigned intermittently from 79 to 192.

it, either has, or soon attains the Spirit of the whole Body. Never was it known, that an *Aristocracy*, which was haughty and tyrannical in one Century, became easy and mild in the next. In effect, the Yoke of this Species of Government is so galling, that whenever the People have got the least Power, they have shaken it off with the utmost Indignation, and established a popular Form. And when they have not had Strength enough to support themselves, they have thrown themselves into the Arms of *Despotism*, as the more eligible of the two Evils. This latter was the Case of *Denmark*, who sought a Refuge from the Oppression of its Nobility, in the strong Hold of arbitrary Power. *Poland* has at present the Name of Republick, and it is one of the *Aristocratick* Form; but it is well known, that the little Finger of this Government, is heavier than the Loins of arbitrary Power in most Nations. The People are not only politically, but personally Slaves, and treated with the utmost Indignity. The Republick of *Venice* is somewhat more moderate; yet even here, so heavy is the *Aristocratick* Yoke, that the Nobles have been obliged to enervate the Spirit of their Subjects by every Sort of Debauchery; they have denied them the Liberty of Reason, and they have made them amends, by what a base Soul will think a more valuable Liberty,[a] by not only

allowing, but encouraging them to corrupt themselves in the most scandalous Manner. They consider their Subjects, as the Farmer does the Hog
he keeps to feast upon. He holds him fast in his
Stye, but allows him to wallow as much as he
pleases in his beloved Filth and Gluttony. So
scandalously debauched a People as that of *Venice*,
is to be met with no where else. High, Low, Men,
Women, Clergy, and Laity, are all alike. The ruling
Nobility are no less afraid of one another, than
they are of the People; and for that Reason, politically enervate their own Body by the same ef-
feminate Luxury, by which they corrupt their Subjects. They are impoverished by every Means
which can be invented; and they are kept in a
perpetual Terror by the Horrors of a State-
inquisition; here you see a People deprived of all
rational Freedom, and tyrannized over by about
two thousand Men; and yet this Body of two
thousand, are so far from enjoying any Liberty by
the Subjection of the rest, that they are in an
infinitely severer State of Slavery; they make
themselves the most degenerate, and unhappy of
Mankind, for no other Purpose than that they
may the more effectually contribute to the Misery
of an whole Nation. In short, the regular and
methodical Proceedings of an *Aristocracy*, are more

intolerable than the very Excesses of a *Despotism,* and in general, much further from any Remedy.

Thus, my Lord, we have pursued *Aristocracy* through its whole Progress; we have seen the Seeds, the Growth, and the Fruit. It could boast none of the Advantages of a *Despotism,* miserable as those Advantages were, and it was overloaded with an Exuberance of Mischiefs, unknown even to *Despotism* itself. In effect, it is no more than a disorderly Tyranny. This Form therefore could be little approved even in Speculation, by those who were capable of thinking, and could be less borne in Practice by any who were capable of feeling. However, the fruitful Policy of Man was not yet exhausted. He had yet another Farthing-candle to supply the Deficiencies of the Sun. This was the third Form, known by political Writers under the Name of *Democracy.* Here the People transacted all publick Business, or the greater Part of it, in their own Persons: their Laws were made by them-selves, and upon any Failure of Duty, their Officers were accountable to themselves, and to them only. In all appearance, they had secured by this Method the Advantages of Order and good Government, without paying their Liberty for the Purchace.[a] Now, my Lord, we are come to the Master-piece of *Grecian* Refinement, and *Roman*

Solidity, a popular Government. The earliest and most celebrated Republic of this Model, was that of *Athens*. It was constructed by no less an Artist, than the celebrated Poet and Philosopher, *Solon*.[42] But no sooner was this political Vessel launched from the Stocks, than it overset, even in the Lifetime of the Builder. A Tyranny immediately supervened;[43] not by a foreign Conquest, not by Accident, but by the very Nature and Constitution of a *Democracy*. An artful Man became popular, the People had Power in their Hands, and they devolved a considerable Share of their Power upon their Favourite; and the only Use he made of this Power, was to plunge those who gave it into Slavery. Accident restored their Liberty, and the same good Fortune produced Men of uncommon Abilities and uncommon Virtues amongst them. But these Abilities were suffered to be of little Service either to their Possessors or to the State. Some of these Men, for whose Sakes alone we read their History, they banished;[a] others they imprisoned; and all they treated with various Circumstances of the most shameful Ingratitude. Republicks have many Things in the

---

[42]Solon (c.639–c.559) reformed the Athenian laws and made them more democratic. Compare n. 31.

[43]Pisistratus (c.605–527) was thrice tyrant of Athens apparently at the demand of the rural populace.

Spirit of absolute Monarchy, but none more than
this; a shining Merit is ever hated or suspected in
a popular Assembly, as well as in a Court; and all
Services done the State, are looked upon as
dangerous to the Rulers, whether Sultans or
Senators. The *Ostracism* at *Athens* was built upon
this Principle. The giddy People, whom we have
now under Consideration, being elated with some
Flashes of Success, which they owed to nothing
less than any Merit of their own, began to tyran-
nize over their Equals, who had associated with
them for their common Defence. With their Pru-
dence they renounced all Appearance of Justice.
They entered into Wars rashly and wantonly. If
they were unsuccessful, instead of growing wiser
by their Misfortune, they threw the whole Blame
of their own Misconduct on the Ministers who
had advised, and the Generals who had conducted those Wars; until by degrees they had cut
off all who could serve them in their Councils or
their Battles. If at any time these Wars had an
happier Issue, it was no less difficult to deal with
them on account of their Pride and Insolence.
Furious in their Adversity, tyrannical in their Suc-
cesses, a Commander had more Trouble to concert
his Defence before the People, than to plan the
Operations of the Campaign. It was not uncommon[a] for a General, under the horrid *Despotism* of

the *Roman* Emperors, to be ill received in proportion to the Greatness of his Services. *Agricola* is a strong Instance of this. No Man had done greater Things, nor with more honest[a] Ambition. Yet on his Return to Court, he was obliged to enter *Rome* with all the Secrecy of a Criminal. He went to the Palace, not like a victorious Commander who had merited and might demand the greatest Rewards, but like an Offender who had come to supplicate a Pardon for his Crimes. His Reception was answerable: *"Brevi osculo, & nullo sermone exceptus, turbæ servientium immistus est."*[44] Yet in that worse Season of this worst of monarchical* Tyrannies, Modesty, Discretion, and a Coolness of Temper, formed some kind of Security even for the highest Merit. But at *Athens,* the nicest and best studied Behaviour was not a sufficient Guard for a Man of great Capacity. Some of their bravest Command-

---

*Sciant quibus moris illicita mirari, posse etiam sub malis principibus magnos viros, etc. See 42 to the End of it.[45]

---

[44]See n. 45.

[45]"With the greeting of a hasty kiss and without conversation, he slipped away into the obsequious mob. [Let those whose way it is to admire only what is forbidden learn from him that great men can live even under bad rulers, etc.]" M. Hutton, rev. R.M. Ogilivie, trans., *Tacitus: Agricola, Germania, Dialogus* (Cambridge, Mass: Harvard University Press, 1970), 40 and 42. Looking at the sections following 42, especially 45, we find that there is some doubt that an upright man can live in corrupt times. It is suggested that had Agricola not died, the emperor Domitian would eventually have killed him. Compare n. 36 of the *Vindication.*

ers were obliged to fly their Country, some to enter into the Service of its Enemies, rather than abide a popular Determination of their Conduct, lest, as one of them said, their Giddiness might make the People condemn where they meant to acquit; to throw in a black Bean, even when they intended a white one.

The *Athenians* made a very rapid Progress to the most enormous Excesses. The People under no Restraint soon grew dissolute, luxurious, and idle. They renounced all Labour, and began to subsist themselves from the publick Revenues. They lost all Concern for their common Honour or Safety, and could bear no Advice that tended to reform them. At this time Truth became offensive to those Lords the People, and most highly dangerous to the Speaker. The Orators no longer ascended the *Rostrum,* but to corrupt them further with the most fulsome Adulation. These Orators were all bribed by foreign Princes on the one Side or the other. And besides its own Parties, in this City there were Parties, and avowed ones too, for the *Persians, Spartans,* and *Macedonians,* supported each of them by one or more Demagogues pensioned and bribed to this iniquitous Service. The People, forgetful of all Virtue and publick Spirit, and intoxicated with the Flatteries of their Orators (these Courtiers of Republicks, and endowed with the distinguishing Characteristicks of all other Courtiers) this People, I say, at last arrived at that Pitch of Madness, that they coolly and deliberately, by an express Law, made it capital for any Man to propose an Application of the immense Sums squandered in publick Shows, even to the most necessary Purposes of the State. When you see the People of this Republick banishing or murdering their best and ablest Citizens, dissipating the publick Treasure with the most senseless Extravagance, and spending their whole Time, as Spectators or Actors, in playing, fiddling, dancing, and singing, does it not, my Lord, strike your Imagination with the Image of a sort of a complex *Nero*? And does it not strike you with the greater Horror, when you observe, not one Man only, but a whole City, grown drunk with Pride and Power, running with a Rage of Folly into the same mean and senseless Debauchery and Extravagance? But if this People resembled *Nero* in their Extravagance, much more did they resemble and even exceed him in Cruelty and Injustice. In the Time of *Pericles*,[46] one of the most celebrated Times in the History of that Commonwealth, a King of *Egypt* sent them a Donation of Corn. This they

---

[46]Compare "Pericles," *The Lives of the Noble Grecians and Romans.*

were mean enough to accept. And had the *Egyptian* Prince intended the Ruin of this City of wicked *Bedlamites*,[47] he could not have taken a more effectual Method to do it, than by such an ensnaring Largess. The Distribution of this Bounty caused a Quarrel; the Majority set on foot an Enquiry into the Title of the Citizens; and upon a vain Pretence of Illegitimacy, newly and occasionally set up, they deprived of their Share of the royal Donation no less than five thousand of their own Body. They went further; they disfranchised them; and having once begun with an Act of Injustice, they could set no Bounds to it. Not content with cutting them off from the Rights of Citizens, they plundered these unfortunate Wretches of all their Substance; and to crown this Masterpiece of Violence and Tyranny, they actually sold every Man of the five thousand as Slaves in the publick Market. Observe, my Lord, that the five thousand we here speak of, were cut off from a Body of no more than nineteen thousand; for the entire Number of Citizens was no greater at that Time. Could the Tyrant who wished the *Roman* People but one Neck; could the Tyrant *Caligula* himself[a] have done, nay, he could scarcely wish for a greater Mischief, than to have cut off, at one

---

[47]See n. 64.

Stroke, a fourth of his People? Or has the Cruelty of that Series of sanguine Tyrants, the *Caesars,* ever presented such a Piece of flagrant and extensive[a] Wickedness? The whole History of this celebrated Republick is but one Tissue of Rashness, Folly, Ingratitude, Injustice, Tumult, Violence, and Tyranny, and indeed of every Species of Wickedness that can well be imagined. This was a City of Wisemen, in which a Minister could not exercise his Functions; a warlike People, amongst whom a General did not dare either to gain or lose a Battle; a learned Nation, in which a Philosopher could not venture on a free Enquiry. This was the City which banished *Themistocles,* starved *Aristides,* forced into Exile *Miltiades,* drove out *Anaxagoras,* and poisoned *Socrates.*[48] This was a City which changed the Form of its Government

---

[48]Whereas the oppression of outstanding men by despotisms is understated (see n. 45), these offenses are somewhat exaggerated. Themistocles (c.525–c.460), the strategic savior of the Greeks from the second Persian invasion, was ostracized, a regular institution used to preserve the democracy from the influence of great men, and then he was accused, apparently unjustly, of conspiring with the Persians against the Greeks. See Plutarch, "Themistocles," *The Lives of the Noble Grecians and Romans.* Aristides (d.c.468), called "the Just," was an Athenian general at Marathon and Salamis, when the Greeks twice repulsed the Persians. Athens did not starve him. He was poor, and it did not feed him perhaps by his own choice. See Plutarch, "Aristides," *The Lives of the Noble Grecians and Romans.* Miltiades (d. 489) was the commanding general at Marathon. He was fined and not exiled. Anaxagoras (c. 500–428) was a Greek philosopher who fled Athens because he claimed that the heavenly bodies were not gods. Socrates (469–399) was condemned to death partly as a result of his unyielding defense. See Plato, *The Apology of Socrates.*

with the Moon; eternal Conspiracies, Revolutions daily, nothing fixed and established. A Republick, as an ancient Philosopher has observed, is no one Species of Government, but a Magazine of every Species;[49] here you find every Sort of it, and that in the worst Form. As there is a perpetual Change, one rising and the other falling, you have all the Violence and wicked Policy, by which a beginning Power must always acquire its Strength, and all the Weakness by which falling States are brought to a complete Destruction.

Rome has a more venerable Aspect than *Athens;* and she conducted her Affairs, so far as related to the Ruin and Oppression of the greatest Part of the World, with greater[a] Wisdom and more Uniformity.[b] But the domestic Oeconomy of these two States[c] was nearly or altogether the same. An internal Dissention constantly tore to Pieces the Bowels of the *Roman* Commonwealth.[d] You find the same Confusion, the same Factions which subsisted at *Athens,* the same Tumults, the same Revolutions, and in fine, the same Slavery. If perhaps their former Condition did not deserve that Name altogether as well. All other Republicks were of the same Character. *Florence* was a Transcript of *Athens.* And the modern Republicks, as

---

[49]Compare Plato, *Republic,* 557d–e.

they approach more or[a] less to the Democratick Form, partake more or less of the Nature of those which I have described.

We are now at the Close of our Review of the three simple Forms of artificial Society, and we have shewn them, however they may differ in Name, or in some slight Circumstances, to be all alike in effect; in effect, to be all Tyrannies. But suppose we were inclined to make the most ample Concessions; let us concede *Athens, Rome, Carthage,*[50] and two or three more of the ancient, and as many[b] of the modern Commonwealths, to have been, or to be free and happy, and to owe their Freedom and Happiness to their political Constitution. Yet allowing all this, what Defence does this make for artificial Society in general, that these inconsiderable Spots of the Globe have for some short Space of Time stood as Exceptions to a Charge so general? But when we call these Governments free, or concede that their Citizens were happier than those which lived under different Forms, it is merely *ex abundanti.* For we should be greatly mistaken, if we really thought that the Majority of the People which filled these

---

[50]The choice of these cities, Athens, a democracy, Rome, a mixture of aristocracy and democracy, and Carthage, according to Aristotle (*Politics,* 1272a–1273b), an oligarchy with elements of aristocracy and democracy, points to the superiority of mixed government.

Cities, enjoyed even that nominal political Freedom of which I have spoken so much already. In
reality, they had no Part of it. In *Athens* there were
usually from ten to thirty thousand Freemen: This
was the utmost. But the Slaves usually amounted
to four hundred thousand, and sometimes to a
great many more. The Freemen of *Sparta* and
Rome were not more numerous in proportion to
those whom they held in a Slavery, even more
terrible than the *Athenian*.[a] Therefore state the
Matter fairly: The free States never formed,
though they were taken all together, the
thousandth Part of the habitable Globe; the
Freemen in these States were never the twentieth
Part of the People, and the Time they subsisted is
scarce any thing in that immense Ocean of Duration in which Time and Slavery are so nearly
commensurate. Therefore call these free States, or
popular Governments, or what you please; when
we consider the Majority of their Inhabitants, and
regard the Natural Rights of Mankind, they must
appear in Reality and Truth, no better than pitiful
and oppressive Oligarchies.[51]

---

[51] The modern free commonwealths, like Venice, are not accused of
having slavery. Although they have economic abuses, they appear to be
an improvement over their ancient counterparts. Perhaps the modern
condition has something to do with the spread of the doctrine of "the
Natural Rights of Mankind"—a remarkable phrase to appear in Burke,
and for the second time. See p. 50.

After so fair an Examen, wherein nothing has been exaggerated; no Fact produced which cannot be proved, and none which has been produced in any wise forced or strained, while thousands have, for Brevity, been omitted; after so candid a Discussion in all respects; what Slave so passive, what Bigot so blind, what Enthusiast so headlong, what Politician so hardened, as to stand up in Defence of a System calculated for a Curse to Mankind? a Curse under which they smart and groan to this Hour, without thoroughly knowing the Nature of the Disease, and wanting Understanding or Courage to apply the Remedy.

I need not excuse myself to your Lordship, nor, I think, to any honest Man, for the Zeal I have shewn in this Cause; for it is an honest Zeal, and in a good Cause. I have defended Natural Religion against a Confederacy of Atheists and Divines.[52] I now plead for Natural Society against Politicians, and for Natural Reason against all three. When the World is in a fitter Temper than it is at present to hear Truth, or when I shall be more indifferent about its Temper; my Thoughts

---

[52]Compare Charles Montesquieu, *Defense de l'Esprit des Lois* [*Defense of* The Spirit of the Laws] ed. Roger Caillois, 2 vols. (Paris: Librairie Gallimard, 1951), 2:1134–36. In response to the tenth objection made to *The Spirit of the Laws*, Montesquieu defends himself in terms very similar to those of the noble writer. He cannot admit to disbelieving the doctrines of the Catholic religion, but in defending himself against this accusation, he does defend natural religion against believers and atheists.

may become more publick. In the mean time, let
them repose in my own Bosom, and in the
Bosoms of such Men as are fit to be initiated in
the sober Mysteries of Truth and Reason. My An-
tagonists have already done as much as I could
desire. Parties in Religion and Politics make
sufficient Discoveries concerning each other, to
give a sober Man a proper Caution against them
all. The Monarchic, Aristocratical, and Popular
Partizans have been jointly laying their Axes to
the Root of all Government, and have in their
Turns proved each other absurd and inconvenient. In vain you tell me that Artificial Government is good, but that I fall out only with the
Abuse. The Thing! the Thing itself is the Abuse!
Observe, my Lord, I pray you, that grand Error
upon which all artificial legislative Power is
founded. It was observed, that Men had ungovernable Passions, which made it necessary to
guard against the Violence they might offer to
each other. They appointed Governors over them
for this Reason; but a worse and more perplexing
Difficulty arises, how to be defended against the
Governors? *Quis custodiet ipsos custodes?* [53] In vain

---

[53]Literally, "Who will guard the guardians?" This quotation is the first
of three from Juvenal's (first to second centuries A.D.) *Satire VI*, lines
346–347. It satirizes women and the relations between the sexes. The
guards referred to by Juvenal are those guarding women, presumably in
a women's quarters. Men do not rely on the virtue of either the women

they change from a single Person to a few. These few have the Passions of the one, and they unite to strengthen themselves, and to secure the Gratification of their lawless Passions at the Expence of the general Good. In vain do we fly to the Many. The Case is worse; their Passions are less under the Government of Reason, they are augmented by the Contagion, and defended against all Attacks by their Multitude.

I have purposely avoided the mention of the mixed Form of Government, for Reasons that will be very obvious to your Lordship. But my Caution can avail me but little. You will not fail to urge it against me in favour of Political Society. You will not fail to shew how the Errors of the several simple Modes are corrected by a Mixture of all of them, and a proper Ballance of the several Powers in such a State. I confess, my Lord, that this has been long a darling Mistake of my own; and that of all the Sacrifices I have made to Truth,

---

or the guards but normally employ eunuchs. Juvenal parodies a question raised by Plato in the *Republic* (403e). Plato saw that even in the best regime with the best educated guardians of the law, there is still a problem insuring that the guardians themselves obey the law.

The introduction of Juvenal indicates that the letter has become somewhat ironic. The Juvenalian quotations occur in the discussions of institutions related to England. See Montesquieu's prediction that England would give rise to many Juvenals before one Horace (*The Spirit of the Laws*, Bk. 19, ch. 27).

this has been by far the greatest. When I confess that I think this Notion a Mistake, I know to whom I am speaking, for I am satisfied that Reasons are like Liquors, and there are some of such a Nature as none but strong Heads can bear. There are few with whom I can communicate so freely as with *Pope*.[54] But *Pope* cannot bear every Truth. He has a Timidity which hinders the full Exertion of his Faculties, almost as effectually as Bigotry cramps those of the general Herd of Mankind. But whoever is a genuine Follower of Truth, keeps his Eye steady upon his Guide, indifferent whither he is led, provided that she is the Leader. And, my Lord, if it be properly considered, it were infinitely better to remain possessed by the whole Legion of vulgar Mistakes, than to reject some, and at the same time to retain a Fondness for others altogether as absurd and irrational. The first has at least a Consistency, that makes a Man, however erroneously, uniform at least; but the latter way of proceeding is such an inconsistent Chimæra and Jumble of Philosophy and vulgar Prejudice, that hardly any thing more ridiculous can be conceived. Let us therefore freely, and

---

[54]Alexander Pope (1688–1744) was an English poet, friend of Bolingbroke, and supposedly a major influence on Montesquieu when he wrote *The Spirit of the Laws*. See n. 52 and n. 66.

without Fear or Prejudice, examine this last Contrivance of Policy. And without considering how near the Quick our Instruments may come, let us search it to the Bottom.

First then, all Men are agreed, that this Junction of Regal, Aristocratic, and Popular Power, must form a very complex, nice, and intricate Machine, which being composed of such a Variety of Parts, with such opposite Tendencies and Movements, it must be liable on every Accident to be disordered. To speak without Metaphor, such a Government must be liable to frequent Cabals, Tumults, and Revolutions, from its very Constitution. These are undoubtedly as ill Effects, as can happen in a Society; for in such a Case, the Closeness acquired by Community, instead of serving for mutual Defence, serves only to increase the Danger. Such a System is like a City, where Trades that require constant Fires are much exercised, where the Houses are built of combustible Materials, and where they stand extremely close.

In the second Place, the several constituent Parts having their distinct Rights, and these many of them so necessary to be determined with Exactness, are yet so indeterminate in their Nature, that it becomes a new and constant Source of Debate and Confusion. Hence it is, that whilst the Business of Government should be carrying on, the Question is, who has a Right to exercise this or that Function of it, or what Men have Power to keep their Offices in any Function. Whilst this Contest continues, and whilst the Ballance in any sort continues, it has never any Remission; all manner of Abuses and Villanies in Officers remain unpunished, the greatest Frauds and Robberies in the publick Revenues are committed in Defiance of Justice; and Abuses grow, by Time and Impunity, into Customs; until they prescribe against the Laws, and grow too inveterate often to admit a Cure, unless such as may be as bad as the Disease.

Thirdly, the several Parts of this Species of Government, though united, preserve the Spirit which each Form has separately. Kings are ambitious; the Nobility haughty; and the Populace tumultuous and ungovernable. Each Party, however in appearance peaceable, carries on a Design upon the others; and it is owing to this, that in all Questions, whether concerning foreign or domestick Affairs, the Whole generally turns more upon some Party-Matter than upon the Nature of the Thing itself; whether such a Step will diminish or augment the Power of the Crown, or how far the Privileges of the Subject are like to be extended or restricted by it. And these Questions are constantly resolved, without any Consideration of the

Merits of the Cause, merely as the Parties who uphold these jarring Interests may chance to prevail; and as they prevail, the Ballance is overset, now upon one side, now upon the other. The Government is one Day, arbitrary Power in a single Person; another, a juggling Confederacy of a few to cheat the Prince and enslave the People; and the third, a frantick and unmanageable Democracy. The great Instrument of all these Changes, and what infuses a peculiar Venom into all of them, is Party. It is of no Consequence what the Principles of any Party, or what their Pretensions are, the Spirit which actuates all Parties is the same; the Spirit of Ambition, of Self-Interest, of Oppression, and Treachery. This Spirit entirely reverses all the Principles which a benevolent Nature has erected within us; all Honesty, all equal Justice, and even the Ties of natural Society, the natural Affections. In a word, my Lord, we have all *seen,* and if any outward Considerations were worthy the lasting Concern of a wise Man, we have some of us *felt,* such Oppression from Party Government as no other Tyranny can parallel. We behold daily the most important Rights, Rights upon which all the others depend; we behold these Rights determined in the last Resort, without the least Attention even to the Appearance or Colour of Justice; we behold this without Emotion, because we have grown up in the constant View of such Practices; and we are not surprised to hear a Man requested to be a Knave and a Traitor, with as much Indifference as if the most ordinary Favour were asked; and we hear this Request refused, not because it is a most unjust and unreasonable Desire, but that this Worthy has already engaged his Injustice to another. These and many more Points I am far from spreading to their full Extent. You are sensible that I do not put forth half my Strength; and you cannot be at a Loss for the Reason. A Man is allowed sufficient Freedom of Thought, provided he knows how to chuse his Subject properly. You may criticise freely upon the *Chinese* Constitution,[55] and observe with as much Severity as you please upon the Absurd Tricks, or destructive Bigotry of the *Bonzees.* But the Scene is changed as you come homeward, and Atheism or Treason may be the Names given in *Britain*, to what would be Reason and Truth if asserted of *China.* I submit to the Condition, and though I have a notorious Advantage before me, I wave the Pursuit. For else, my Lord, it is very obvious what a Picture might be drawn of the Excesses of

---

[55]Compare Montesquieu, *The Spirit of the Laws,* Bk. 7, chs. 6, 7; Bk. 8, ch. 21; Bk. 9, ch. 8; and especially Bk. 19, chs. 10, 11, 12, 19, 20. Montesquieu praises the Chinese for lying and formulates his famous axiom "that all political vices are not moral vices, and all moral vices are not political vices." Bk. 19, ch. 10.

Party even in our own Nation. I could shew, that
the same Faction has in one Reign promoted
popular Seditions, and in the next been a Patron
of Tyranny; I could shew, that they have all of
them betrayed the publick Safety at all Times, and
have very frequently with equal Perfidy made a
Market of their own Cause, and their own Associates. I could shew how vehemently they have
contended for Names, and how silently they
passed over Things of the last importance. And I
could demonstrate, that they have had the
Opportunity of doing all this Mischief, nay, that
they themselves had their Origin and Growth
from that Complex Form of Government which
we are wisely taught to look upon as so great a
Blessing. Revolve, my Lord, our History from the
Conquest. We scarce ever had a Prince, who by
Fraud, or Violence, had not made some Infringement on the Constitution. We scarce ever had a
Parliament which knew, when it attempted to set
Limits to the Royal Authority, how to set Limits to
its own. Evils we have had continually calling for
Reformation, and Reformations more grievous
than any Evils. Our boasted Liberty sometimes
trodden down, sometimes giddily set up, ever
precariously fluctuating and unsettled; it has been
only kept alive by the Blasts of continual Feuds,
Wars, and Conspiracies. In no Country in *Europe*

has the Scaffold so often blushed with the Blood of its Nobility. Confiscations, Banishments, Attainders, and Executions, make a large Part of the History of such of our Families as are not utterly extinguished by them. Formerly indeed Things had a more ferocious Appearance than they have at this Day. In these early and unrefined Ages, the jarring Parts of a certain chaotic Constitution supported their several Pretensions by the Sword. Experience and Policy have since taught other Methods.

Res vero nunc agitur tenui pulmone rubetæ.[56] But how far Corruption, Venality, the Contempt of Honour, the Oblivion of all Duty to our Country, and the most abandoned publick Prostitution, are preferable to the more glaring and violent Effects of Faction, I will not presume to determine. Sure I am that they are very great Evils.

I have done with the Forms of Government. During the Course of my Enquiry you may have observed a very material Difference between my Manner of Reasoning and that which is in Use amongst the Abetors[a] of artificial Society. They form their Plans upon what seems most eligible to

---

[56]"Whereas nowadays a slice of a toad's lung will do the business." Juvenal, *Satire VI* in *Juvenal and Persius,* trans. G.G. Ramsay (Cambridge, Mass.: Harvard University Press, 1957), line 659. The quotation is a reference to the invention and perfection by women of the art of poisoning.

their Imaginations, for the ordering of Mankind.[57] I discover the Mistakes in those Plans, from the real known Consequences which have resulted from them. They have inlisted Reason to fight against itself, and employ its whole Force to prove that it is an insufficient Guide to them in the Conduct of their Lives. But unhappily for us, in proportion as we have deviated from the plain Rule of our Nature, and turned our Reason against itself, in that Proportion have we increased the Follies and Miseries of Mankind. The more deeply we penetrate into the Labyrinth of Art, the further we find ourselves from those Ends for which we entered it.[58] This has happened in almost every Species of Artificial Society, and in all Times. We found, or we thought we found, an Inconvenience in having every Man the Judge of his own Cause. Therefore Judges were set up, at first with discretionary Powers. But it was soon found a miserable Slavery to have our Lives and Properties precarious, and hanging upon the arbitrary Determination of any one Man, or Set of Men. We flew to Laws as a Rem-

---

[57]Compare Machiavelli, *The Prince*, ch. 15, where he accuses Plato of establishing imaginary republics. The noble writer accuses all legislators, ancient and modern, of the same practice.

[58]The whole discussion of law seems to be an attack on Locke's solution to the inconveniences of the state of nature. Compare *The Second Treatise of Government*, sects. 13 and 20, and ch. 9.

edy for this Evil. By these we persuaded ourselves we might know with some Certainty upon
what Ground we stood. But lo! Differences arose
upon the Sense and Interpretation of these Laws.
Thus we were brought back to our old Incer-
titude. New Laws were made to expound the old;
and new Difficulties arose upon the new Laws; as
Words multiplied, Opportunities of cavilling upon
them multiplied also. Then Recourse was had to
Notes, Comments, Glosses, Reports, *Responsa
Prudentum*, learned Readings: Eagle stood against
Eagle: Authority was set up against Authority.
Some were allured by the modern, others rev-
erenced the ancient. The new were more
enlightened, the old were more venerable. Some
adopted the Comment, others stuck to the Text.
The Confusion increased, the Mist thickened,
until it could be discovered no longer what was
allowed or forbidden, what Things were in Property, and what common. In this Uncertainty,
(uncertain even to the Professors, an *Ægyptian*
Darkness to the rest of Mankind) the contending
Parties felt themselves more effectually ruined by
the Delay than they could have been by the Injustice of any Decision. Our Inheritances are become
a Prize for Disputation; and Disputes and Litiga-
tions are become an Inheritance.

The Professors of Artificial Law have always

walked hand in hand with the Professors of Artificial Theology. As their End, in confounding the Reason of Man, and abridging his natural Freedom, is exactly the same, they have adjusted the Means to that End in a Way entirely similar. The Divine thunders out his *Anathemas* with more Noise and Terror against the Breach of one of his positive Institutions, or the Neglect of some of his trivial Forms, than against the Neglect or Breach of those Duties and Commandments of natural Religion, which by these Forms and Institutions he pretends to enforce. The Lawyer has his Forms, and his positive Institutions too, and he adheres to them with a Veneration altogether as religious. The worst Cause cannot be so prejudicial to the Litigant, as his Advocate's or Attorney's Ignorance or Neglect of these Forms. A Law-suit is like an ill-managed Dispute, in which the first Object is soon out of Sight, and the Parties end upon a Matter wholly foreign to that on which they began. In a Law-suit the Question is, Who has a Right to a certain House or Farm? And this Question is daily determined, not upon the Evidences of the Right, but upon the Observance or Neglect of some Forms of Words in use with the Gentlemen of the Robe, about which[a] there is even amongst themselves such a Disagreement, that the most experienced Veterans in the Profession can never be positively assured that they are not mistaken.

Let us expostulate with these learned Sages, these Priests of the sacred Temple of Justice. Are we Judges of our own Property? By no means. You then, who are initiated into the Mysteries of the blindfold Goddess, inform me whether I have a Right to eat the Bread I have earned by the Hazard of my Life, or the Sweat of my Brow? The grave Doctor answers me in the Affirmative. The reverend Serjeant replies in the Negative; the learned Barrister reasons upon one side and upon the other, and concludes nothing. What shall I do? An Antagonist starts up and presses me hard. I enter the Field, and retain^a these three Persons to defend my Cause. My Cause, which two Farmers from the Plough could have decided in half an Hour, takes the Court twenty Years. I am however at the end of my Labour, and have in Reward for all my Toil and Vexation, a Judgment in my Favour. But hold—a sagacious Commander, in the Adversary's Army has found a Flaw in the Proceeding. My Triumph is turned into Mourning. I have used *or,* instead of *and,* or some Mistake, small in Appearance, but dreadful in its Consequences, and have the whole of my Success quashed in a Writ of Error. I remove my Suit; I shift from Court to Court; I fly from Equity to

Law, and from Law to Equity; equal Uncertainty attends me every where: And a Mistake in which I had no Share, decides at once upon my Liberty and Property, sending me from the Court to a Prison, and adjudging my Family to Beggary and Famine. I am innocent, Gentlemen, of the Darkness and Uncertainty of your Science. I never darkened it with absurd and contradictory Notions, nor confounded it with Chicane and Sophistry. You have excluded me from any Share in the Conduct of my own Cause; the Science was too deep for me; I acknowledged it; but it was too deep even for yourselves: You have made the way so intricate, that you are yourselves lost in it: You err, and you punish me for your Errors.

The Delay of the Law is, your Lordship will tell me, a trite Topic, and which of its Abuses have not been too severely felt not to be often complained of? A Man's Property is to serve for the Purposes of his Support; and therefore to delay a Determination concerning that, is the worst Injustice, because it cuts off the very End and Purpose for which I applied to the Judicature for Relief. Quite contrary in Case of a Man's Life, there the Determination can hardly be too much protracted. Mistakes in this Case are as often fallen into as in any other, and if the Judgment is sudden, the Mistakes are the most irretrievable of all others.

Of this the Gentlemen of the Robe are themselves sensible, and they have brought it into a Maxim. *De morte hominis nulla est cunctatio longa.*[59] But what could have induced them to reverse the Rules, and to contradict that Reason which dictated them, I am utterly unable to guess. A Point concerning Property, which ought, for the Reasons I just mentioned, to be most speedily decided, frequently exercises the Wit of Successions of Lawyers, for many Generations. *Multa virum volvens durando sæcula vincit.*[60] But the Question concerning a Man's Life, that great Question in which no Delay ought to be counted tedious, is commonly determined in twenty-four Hours at the utmost. It is not to be wondered at, that Injustice and Absurdity should be inseparable Companions.

Ask of Politicians the End for which Laws were originally designed; and they will answer, that the Laws were designed as a Protection for the Poor and Weak against the Oppression of the Rich and

---

[59]"No delay can be too long when a man's life is at stake." Juvenal, *Satire VI* in *Juvenal and Persius,* trans. G.G. Ramsay, line 221. This is a husband's reply to a wife who wants a slave crucified for apparently no good reason.

[60]"Many a generation, many an age of man rolls onward and [it] survives them all." Virgil, *Georgic II* in *The Poems of Virgil,* trans. James Rhoades, *The Great Books of the Western World* (Chicago: Encyclopaedia Britannica, 1952), line 295. Virgil describes a tree that is more enduring than men.

Powerful.[61] But surely no Pretence can be so ridiculous; a Man might as well tell me he has taken off my Load, because he has changed the Burthen.[62] If the poor Man is not able to support his Suit, according to the vexatious and expensive manner established in civilized Countries, has not the Rich as great an Advantage over him as the Strong has over the Weak in a State of Nature? But we will not place the State of Nature, which is the Reign of God, in competition with Political Society, which is the absurd Usurpation of Man. In a State of Nature, it is true, that a Man of superior Force may beat or rob me; but then it is true, that I am at full Liberty to defend myself, or make Reprisal by Surprize or by Cunning, or by any other way in which I may be superior to him. But in Political Society, a rich Man may rob me in another way. I cannot defend myself; for Money is the only Weapon with which we are allowed to fight. And if I attempt to avenge myself, the whole Force of that Society is ready to complete[a] my Ruin.

A good Parson once said, that where Mystery begins, Religion ends. Cannot I say, as truly at

---

[61]In Rousseau's *Second Discourse,* the speech that the founder of civil society makes to persuade others to join is essentially the same one that the noble writer here claims politicians make to justify civil society. See *The First and Second Discourses,* pp. 159–62.

[62]Burden.

least, of human Laws, that where Mystery begins, Justice ends? It is hard to say, whether the Doctors of Law or Divinity have made the greater Advances in the lucrative Business of Mystery. The Lawyers, as well as the Theologians, have erected another Reason besides Natural Reason; and the Result has been, another Justice besides Natural Justice. They have so bewildered the World and themselves in unmeaning Forms and Ceremonies, and so perplexed the plainest Matters with metaphysical Jargon, that it carries the highest Danger to a Man out of that Profession, to make the least Step without their Advice and Assistance. Thus by confining to themselves the knowledge of the Foundation of all Men's Lives and Properties, they have reduced all Mankind into the most abject and servile Dependence. We are Tenants at the Will of these Gentlemen for every thing; and a metaphysical Quibble is to decide whether the greatest Villain breathing shall meet his Desserts, or escape with Impunity, or whether the best Man in the Society shall not be reduced to the lowest and most despicable Condition it affords. In a word, my Lord, the Injustice, Delay, Puerility, false Refinement, and affected Mystery of the Law are such, that many who live under it come to admire and envy the Expedition, Simplicity, and Equality of arbitrary Judgments. I need insist the less on this Article to your Lordship, as you have frequently lamented the Miseries derived to us from Artificial Law, and your Candor is the more to be admired and applauded in this, as your Lordship's noble House has derived its Wealth and its Honours from that Profession.

Before we finish our Examination of Artificial Society, I shall lead your Lordship into a closer Consideration of the Relations which it gives Birth to, and the Benefits, if such they are, which result from these Relations. The most obvious Division of Society is into Rich and Poor; and it is no less obvious, that the Number of the former bear a great Disproportion to those of the latter. The whole Business of the Poor is to administer to the Idleness, Folly, and Luxury of the Rich; and that of the Rich, in return, is to find the best Methods of confirming the Slavery and increasing the Burthens of the Poor. In a State of Nature, it is an invariable Law, that a Man's Acquisitions are in proportion to his Labours. In a State of Artificial Society, it is a Law as constant and as invariable, that those who labour most, enjoy the fewest Things; and that those who labour not at all, have the greatest Number of Enjoyments. A Constitution of Things this, strange and ridiculous beyond Expression. We scarce believe a thing when we are told it, which we actually see before our Eyes every Day without being in the least surprized. I suppose that there are in *Great-Britain* upwards of an hundred thousand People employed in Lead, Tin, Iron, Copper, and Coal Mines; these unhappy Wretches scarce ever see the Light of the Sun; they are buried in the Bowels of the Earth; there they work at a severe and dismal Task, without the least Prospect of being delivered from it; they subsist upon the coarsest and worst sort of Fare; they have their Health miserably impaired, and their Lives cut short, by being perpetually confined in the close Vapour of these malignant Minerals. An hundred thousand more at least are tortured without Remission by the suffocating Smoak, intense Fires, and constant Drudgery necessary in refining and managing the Products of those Mines. If any Man informed us that two hundred thousand innocent Persons were condemned to so intolerable Slavery, how should we pity the unhappy Sufferers, and how great would be our just Indignation against those who inflicted so cruel and ignominious a Punishment? This is an Instance, I could not wish a stronger, of the numberless Things which we pass by in their common Dress, yet which shock us when they are nakedly represented. But this Number, considerable as it is, and the Slavery, with all its Baseness and Horror, which we have at home, is nothing to what the rest of the World affords of the same Nature. Millions daily bathed in the poisonous Damps and destructive Effluvia of Lead, Silver, Copper, and Arsenic. To say nothing of those other Employments, those Stations of Wretchedness and Contempt in which Civil Society has placed the numerous *Enfans perdus*[63] of her Army. Would any rational Man submit to one of the most tolerable of these Drudgeries, for all the artificial Enjoyments which Policy has made to result from them? By no means. And yet need I suggest to your Lordship, that those who find the Means, and those who arrive at the End, are not at all the same Persons. On considering the strange and unaccountable Fancies and Contrivances of artificial Reason, I have somewhere called this Earth the Bedlam of our System. Looking now upon the Effects of some of those Fancies, may we not with equal Reason call it likewise the Newgate, and the Bridewell of the Universe.[64] Indeed the Blindness of one Part of Mankind co-operating with the Frenzy and Villainy of the other, has been the real Builder of this respectable Fabric of political Society: And as the

---

[63]Lost children.

[64]Bedlam was the popular name for Bethlehem Royal Hospital, Britain's oldest institution for the mentally ill. Newgate was a prison in London and originally part of the gatehouse of the west gate of London. Bridewell also was a prison.

Blindness of Mankind[a] has caused their Slavery, in Return their State of Slavery is made a Pretence for continuing them in a State of Blindness; for the Politician will tell you gravely, that their Life of Servitude disqualifies the greater Part of the Race of Man[b] for a Search of Truth, and supplies them with no other than mean and insufficient Ideas. This is but too true; and this is one of the Reasons for which I blame such Institutions.

In a Misery of this Sort, admitting some few Lenities, and those too but a few, nine Parts in ten of the whole Race of Mankind drudge through Life. It may be urged perhaps, in palliation of this, that, at least, the rich Few find a considerable and real Benefit from the Wretchedness of the Many. But is this so in fact? Let us examine the Point with a little more Attention. For this Purpose the Rich in all Societies may be thrown into two Classes. The first is of those who are Powerful as well as Rich, and conduct the Operations of the vast political Machine. The other is of those who employ their Riches wholly in the Acquisition of Pleasure. As to the first Sort, their continual Care, and Anxiety, their toilsome Days, and sleepless Nights, are next to proverbial. These Circumstances are sufficient almost to level their Condition to that of the unhappy Majority; but there are other Circumstances which place them in a far lower Condition. Not only their Understandings labour continually, which is the severest Labour, but their Hearts are torn by the worst, most troublesome, and insatiable of all Passions, by Avarice, by Ambition, by Fear and Jealousy. No part of the Mind has Rest. Power gradually extirpates from the Mind every humane and gentle Virtue. Pity, Benevolence, Friendship are Things almost unknown in high Stations. *Varæ amicitiæ rarissime inveniuntur in iis qui in honoribus reque publica*[a] *versantur,* says *Cicero.*[65] And indeed, Courts are the Schools where Cruelty, Pride, Dissimulation, and Treachery are studied and taught in the most vicious Perfection. This is a Point so clear and acknowledged, that if it did not make a necessary Part of my Subject, I should pass it by entirely. And this has hindered me from drawing at full length, and in the most striking Colours, this shocking Picture of the Degeneracy and Wretchedness of human Nature, in that Part which is vulgarly thought its happiest and most amiable State. You know from what Originals I could copy such Pictures. Happy are they who know enough

---

[65]"True friendships are very hard to find among those whose time is spent in office or in business of a public kind." W. A. Falconer, trans., *De amicitia* in *Cicero: De senectus, De amicitia, De divinatione* (Cambridge, Mass.: Harvard University Press, 1938), pp. xvii, 64. Cicero, throughout *De amicitia,* describes a friendship between two political men—Caius Laelius and Scipio Africanus.

of them to know the little Value of the Possessors
of such Things, and of all that they possess; and
happy they who[a] have been snatched from that
Post of Danger which they occupy, with the Re-
mains of their Virtue; Loss of Honours, Wealth,
Titles, and even the Loss of one's Country, is
nothing in Balance[b] with so great an Advantage.

Let us now view the other Species of the Rich,
those who devote their Time and Fortunes to
Idleness and Pleasure. How much happier are
they? The Pleasures which are agreeable to Nature
are within the reach of all, and therefore can form
no Distinction in favour of the Rich. The Pleasures
which Art forces up are seldom sincere, and never
satisfying. What is worse, this constant Application to Pleasure takes away from the Enjoyment,
or rather turns it into the Nature of a very bur-
thensome and laborious Business. It has Consequences much more fatal.[c] It produces a weak
valetudinary State of Body, attended by all those
horrid Disorders, and yet more horrid Methods of
Cure, which are the Result of Luxury on one
hand, and the weak and ridiculous Efforts of
human Art on the other. The Pleasures of such
Men[d] are scarcely felt as Pleasures; at the same
time that they bring on Pains and Diseases, which
are felt but too severely. The Mind has its Share of
the Misfortune; it grows lazy and enervate, un-

willing and unable to search for Truth, and utterly uncapable of knowing, much less of relishing real Happiness. The Poor by their excessive Labour, and the Rich by their enormous Luxury, are set upon a Level, and rendered[a] equally ignorant of any Knowledge which might conduce to their Happiness. A dismal View of the Interior of all Civil Society. The lower Part broken and ground down by the most cruel Oppression; and the Rich by their artificial Method of Life bringing worse Evils on themselves, than their Tyranny could possibly inflict on those below them. Very different is the Prospect of the Natural State. Here there are no Wants[b] which Nature gives, and in this State Men can be sensible of no other Wants, which are not to be supplied by a very moderate Degree of Labour; therefore there is no Slavery. Neither is there any Luxury, because no single Man can supply the Materials of it. Life is simple, and therefore it is happy.

I am conscious, my Lord, that your Politician will urge in his Defence, that this unequal State is highly useful. That without dooming some Part of Mankind to extraordinary Toil, the Arts which cultivate Life could not be exercised. But I demand of this Politician, how such Arts came to be necessary? He answers, that Civil Society could not well exist without them. So that these Arts are necessary to Civil Society, and Civil Society necessary again to these Arts. Thus running in a Circle, without Modesty, and without End, and making one Error and Extravagance an Excuse for the other. My Sentiments about these Arts and their Cause, I have often discoursed with my Friends at large. *Pope* has expressed them in good Verse, where he talks with so much Force of Reason and Elegance of Language in Praise of the State of Nature:

> Then was not Pride, nor Arts that Pride to aid,
> Man walk'd with Beast, Joint-tenant of the Shade.[66]

On the whole, my Lord, if Political Society, in whatever Form, has still made the Many the Property of the Few; if it has introduced Labours unnecessary, Vices and Diseases unknown, and Pleasures incompatible with Nature; if in all Countries it abridges the Lives of Millions, and renders those of Millions more utterly abject and miserable, shall we still worship so destructive an Idol, and daily sacrifice to it our Health, our Liberty, and our Peace? Or shall we pass by this monstrous Heap of absurd Notions, and abominable Practices, thinking we have sufficiently discharged our Duty in exposing the trifling Cheats,

---

[66]Alexander Pope, *Essay on Man,* Epistle 3, lines 151–52. In the original it reads, "Pride then was not; nor Arts, that Pride to Aid: Man walk'd with beast, joint tenant of the shade."

and ridiculous Juggles of a few mad, designing, or ambitious Priests? Alas! my Lord, we labour under a mortal Consumption, whilst we are so anxious about the Cure of a sore Finger. For has not this Leviathan of Civil Power[67] overflowed the Earth with a Deluge of Blood, as if he were made to disport and play therein? We have shewn, that Political Society, on a moderate Calculation, has been the Means of murdering several times[a] the Number of Inhabitants now upon the Earth, during its short Existence, not upwards of four thousand Years in any Accounts to be depended on. But we have said nothing of the other, and perhaps as bad Consequence of these Wars, which have spilled such Seas of Blood, and reduced so many Millions to a merciless Slavery. But these are only the Ceremonies performed in the Porch of the political Temple. Much more horrid ones are seen as you enter it. The several Species of Government vie with each other in the Absurdity of their Constitutions, and the Oppression which they make their Subjects endure. Take them under what Form you please, they are in effect but a Despotism, and they fall,[b] both in Effect and Appearance too, after a very short Period, into that cruel and detestable Species of Tyranny; which I rather call it, because we have

---

[67]Compare Thomas Hobbes, *Leviathan*, "The Introduction."

been educated under another Form,[68] than that this is of worse Consequences to Mankind. For the free Governments, for the Point of their Space, and the Moment of their Duration, have felt more Confusion, and committed more flagrant Acts of Tyranny, than the most perfect despotic Governments which we have ever known. Turn your Eye next to the Labyrinth of the Law, and the Iniquity conceived in its intricate Recesses. Consider the Ravages committed in the Bowels of all Commonwealths by Ambition, by Avarice, Envy, Fraud, open Injustice, and pretended Friendship; Vices which could draw little Support from a State of Nature, but which blossom and flourish in the Rankness of political Society. Revolve our whole Discourse; add to it all those Reflections which your own good Understanding shall suggest, and make a strenuous Effort beyond the Reach of vulgar Philosophy, to confess that the Cause of Artificial Society is more defenceless even than that of Artificial Religion; that it is as derogatory from the Honour of the

---

[68]The noble writer almost at the last questions the adequacy of the scheme of governments used in the *Vindication*. It is clearly modern, that is, originating with Machiavelli (*Discourses*, Bk. 1, ch. 2, Bk. 2, ch. 2, Bk. 3, ch. 6). Locke uses tyranny to designate governments not protecting the natural rights of man. See *The Second Treatise of Government*, ch. 18. Montesquieu divides the rule of one into monarchy and despotism, calls the rule of more than one a republic, and divides republics into aristocracies, the rule of the few, and democracies, the rule of the many. See *The Spirit of the Laws*, Bk. 2, chs. 2, 3.

Creator, as subversive of human Reason, and productive of infinitely more Mischief to the human Race.

If pretended Revelations have caused Wars where they were opposed, and Slavery where they were received, the pretended wise Inventions of Politicians have done the same. But the Slavery has been much heavier, the Wars far more bloody, and both more universal by many Degrees. Shew me any Mischief produced by the Madness or Wickedness of Theologians, and I will shew you an hundred, resulting from the Ambition and Villainy of Conquerors and Statesmen. Shew me an Absurdity in Religion, I will undertake to shew you an hundred for one in political Laws and Institutions. If you say, that Natural Religion is a sufficient Guide without the foreign Aid of Revelation, on what Principle should Political Laws become necessary? Is not the same Reason available in Theology and in Politics? If the Laws of Nature are the Laws of God, is it consistent with the Divine Wisdom to prescribe Rules to us, and leave the Enforcement of them to the Folly of human Institutions?[69] Will you follow Truth but to a certain Point?

We are indebted for all our Miseries to our Distrust of that Guide, which Providence thought

---

[69]Compare Pope, *Essay on Man*, Epistle 3, lines 144–50.

sufficient for our Condition, our own natural Reason, which rejecting both in human and divine
Things, we have given our Necks to the Yoke of
political and theological Slavery. We have renounced the Prerogative of Man, and it is no
Wonder[a] that we should be treated like Beasts.
But our Misery is much greater than theirs,[b] as
the Crime we commit in rejecting the lawful
Dominion of our Reason is greater than any
which they can commit.[c] If after all, you should
confess all these Things, yet plead the Necessity
of political Institutions, weak and wicked as they
are, I can argue with equal, perhaps superior
Force concerning the Necessity of artificial Religion; and every Step you advance in your Argument, you add a Strength to mine. So that if we
are resolved to submit our Reason and our Liberty
to civil Usurpation, we have nothing to do but to
conform as quietly as we can to the vulgar Notions which are connected with this, and take up
the Theology of the Vulgar[d] as well as their Politics. But if we think this Necessity rather imaginary than real, we should renounce their Dreams
of Society, together with their Visions of Religion,
and vindicate ourselves into perfect Liberty.[70]

---

[70]This is the only instance in the letter, apart from the title, where a
form of the word, "vindication" appears. Compare Locke, *The Second
Treatise of Government*, sects. 4–6.

You are, my Lord, but just entering into the World; I am going out of it. I have played long enough to be heartily tired of the Drama. Whether I have acted my Part in it well or ill, Posterity will judge with more Candor than I, or than the present Age, with our present Passions, can possibly pretend to. For my part, I quit it without a Sigh, and submit to the Sovereign Order without murmuring. The nearer we approach to the Goal of Life, the better we begin to understand the true Value of our Existence, and the real Weight of our Opinions. We set out much in love with both; but we leave much behind us as we advance. We first throw away the Tales along with the Rattles of our Nurses; those of the Priest keep their Hold a little longer; those of our Governors the longest of all. But the Passions which prop these Opinions are withdrawn one after another; and the cool Light of Reason at the Setting of our Life, shews us what a false Splendor played upon these Objects during our more sanguine Seasons. Happy, my Lord, if instructed by my Experience, and even by my Errors, you come early to make such an Estimate of Things, as may give Freedom and Ease to your Life. I am happy that such an Estimate[a] promises me Comfort at my Death.

FINIS.

TEXTUAL VARIANTS

All variants, with one exception, which is noted, are from the 1756 first edition. The first variant listed is the "Advertisement" to the first edition.

Page 3,a.   ADVERTISEMENT.
The following Letter appears to have been written about the Year 1748, and the Person to whom it is addressed need not be pointed out. As it is probable the Noble Writer had no Design that it should ever appear in Publick, this will account for his having kept no Copy of it, and consequently, for its not appearing amongst the rest of his Works. By what Means it came into the Hands of the Editor, is not at all material to the Publick, any farther than as such an Account might tend to authenticate the Genuineness of it, and for this it was thought it might safely rely on its own internal Evidence.

Page 14,a.   . . . Affections, the Children . . .

Page 21,a.   . . . only consider Peace as a breathing Time . . .

Page 21,b.   . . . are but Accounts of their Butcheries of each other.

Page 22,a.   . . . Provision he must have been subject to . . .

Page 23,a.   . . . of the World. If this was the . . .

Page 23,b.   . . . the Conquered, those Nations who lost their Liberty, and those who fought for it together, must have had a much heavier Loss. They must have lost at least double that Number, as the greatest Slaughter . . .

Page 23,c.   . . . Rage of Conquest. This Conqueror, the oldest . . .

Page 23,d.   . . . opens . . .

Page 23,e.   . . . 1,800,000 . . .

Page 25,a.   We hear of her Army of above three Millions employed in a War against the *Indians*. We hear of their having a yet greater; and of a War continued with much fury, and with various Success. This ends in an Account of her Retreat, with scarce . . .

Page 25,b.   . . . equal Sufferer. Its Loss must in this way of Computation be two Millions more. So that in this . . .

Page 25,c.   . . . she . . .
Page 25,d.   . . . four Millions . . .
Page 26,a.   . . . draining . . .
Page 26,b.   . . . its . . .
Page 26,c.   . . . its . . .
Page 27,a.   . . . three Millions.
Page 28,a.   . . . Divisions, to say nothing of their . . .
Page 30,a.   . . . embraced . . .
Page 30,b.   . . . five Millions . . .
Page 30,c.   The *Mithridatick* War . . .
Page 31,a.   The same Commander . . .
Page 31,b.   The same Prince . . .
Page 35,a.   . . . forty Millions.
Page 35,b.   . . . slain in Battles, from the beginning . . .
Page 35,c.   . . . only at . . .
Page 36,a.   . . . a trifling Calculation . . .
Page 37,a.   . . . to your Lordship. I have no need to exaggerate . . .
Page 38,a.   . . . 40 Millions. I suppose a thousand times as many killed
in Battles. But I must make another Addition not less than the former,
for the Consequences of Wars, in Skirmishes, Massacres, the contagi-
ous Disorders, and the Famine which attend them, more destructive
than Battles themselves. So that allowing me in my Exuberance one
way for my Deficiencies in others, I rate the Destruction caused by
War, at eighty thousand Millions.
Page 38,b.   . . . 160 times . . .
Page 38,c.   But to give . . .
Page 38,d.   . . . charging to Political . . .
Page 38,e.   . . . attended with so deplorable Consequences.
Page 38,f.   In a State of Nature, it would be impossible to join to-
gether a Number of Men, sufficiently agreed in the same bloody De-
sign, necessary to make a very extensive Havock of their Species; and
if they would come to such an Agreement . . .
Page 38,g.   . . . a Purpose . . .
Page 39,a.   . . . too . . .
Page 39,b.   . . . Ruining . . .
Page 39,c.   . . . at . . .
Page 39,d.   . . . even of those . . .
Page 41,a.   . . . than that they were another Combination of People,
and called by another Name . . .
Page 41,b.   Would you inspire this Compatriot of ours with Pity or Re-
gard, for one of these? Would you not hide that Distinction?
Page 41,c.   . . . to Nature . . .
Page 42,a.   . . . the Name applied . . .
Page 42,b.   . . . this . . .
Page 43,a.   . . . I should say . . .

Page 44,a.   . . . but I can have but a very humble Opinion of Institu-
tions . . .
Page 45,a.   So that neglecting the publick Welfare . . .
Page 46,a.   . . . to rule . . .
Page 49,a.   Nay, even . . .
Page 51,a.   . . . Societies, most . . .
Page 52,a.   . . . debarred; this Prospect . . .
Page 52,b.   . . . their . . .
Page 52,c.   . . . and Dread . . .
Page 53,a.   . . . Reason, and have recompensed it . . .
Page 55,a.   . . . Purchase.
Page 56,a.   . . . State. Some they banished . . .
Page 57,a.   It was frequent enough . . .
Page 58,a.   . . . with an honester . . .
Page 61,a.   . . . Tyrant himself . . .
Page 62,a.   . . . entensive (1757) . . .
Page 63,a.   . . . more . . .
Page 63,b.   . . . more Uniformity.
Page 63,c.   But their domestick Oeconomy was . . .
Page 63,d.   . . . of this Commonwealth.
Page 64,a.   . . . of . . .
Page 64,b.   . . . and many . . .
Page 65,a.   . . . the *Athenians.*
Page 75,a.   . . . Abbetors . . .
Page 78,a.   . . . in Use amongst them, amongst which there . . .
Page 79,a.   . . . return . . .
Page 82,a.   . . . compleat . . .
Page 87,a.   . . . as their Blindness has . . .
Page 87,b.   . . . disqualifies them for a . . .
Page 88,a.   . . . *honoribus reipublicæ* . . .
Page 89,a.   . . . know enough of them to know their little Value, and
who have . . .
Page 89,b.   . . . Ballance . . .
Page 89,c.   . . . Consequences yet worse.
Page 89,d.   Their Pleasures are . . .
Page 90,a.   . . . made . . .
Page 90,b.   . . . is no want which . . .
Page 92,a.   . . . murdering an hundred and forty times . . .
Page 92,b.   . . . and fall . . .
Page 95,a.   . . . is not wonderful . . .
Page 95,b.   . . . much the greater, as . . .
Page 95,c.   . . . is greater. If after all . . .
Page 95,d.   . . . take up their Theology as well . . .
Page 96,a.   . . . that it promises . . .

INDEX

Power (*cont.*)
  error underlying legislative,
    67–68
  of the rich, 82, 87–89
Prince, The (Machiavelli), 20*n*, 40*n*,
    76*n*
Property, judicial decisions regard-
    ing, 80–81
Punic Wars, 30

Reason, 17, 76, 78, 94
  rejection of, 95
Religion, 17
  artificial, *xxi–xxii*, 18, 44–45,
    93–95
  civil society and, *xxi–xxii*, 17–19
  natural, *xxi*, 44, 66, 78, 94
  revealed, *xxi*, 18, 94
Religious wars, 35*n*
Republic (Plato), 68*n*
Republics, 52–54, 56–57, 60, 62–64,
    93*n*
Revealed religion, *xxi*, 18, 94
Rich, the, 84, 87–90
  laws and, 82
  pleasure-seeking, 89–90
  power-seeking, 87–89
Rights
  governmental infringement of,
    43
  judicial determination of, 78–79
  natural, 65
  party government and, 72
Roman Empire, 28–32, 34*n*, 58
Rome, 63–65
Rousseau, Jean-Jacques, 15*n*, 21*n*,
    82*n*

St. John, Henry. *See* Bolingbroke,
    Viscount
Scythians, 22*n*, 24*n*
Second Treatise of Government, The
    (Locke), 14*n*, 15*n*, 24*n*, 50*n*,
    51*n*, 76*n*, 93*n*, 95*n*
Self-defense, 82

Semiramis, 24–25
Seneca, 46*n*
Servile wars (ancient Rome), 31–32
Sesostris, 22–24
Sesostris I, 22*n*
Sicily, 28–29
Slavery, 40, 90, 94, 95
  aristocracies and, 51, 53, 54
  in Athens, 56, 61, 65
  despotism and, 45, 49
  of the poor, 84–87
  in Rome, 63, 65
Social war (ancient Rome), 31–32
Society
  artificial. *See* Artificial society
  civil. *See* Civil society
  foundations of, *xix*, *xx*, 11
  natural, *xix–xx*, 15, 66
  political. *See* Political society
Socrates, 62
Solon, 56
Spanish wars, 31–32
Sparta, 65
Specious arguments, 5–9
Spirit of the Laws, The (Mon-
    tesquieu), 12*n*, 16*n*, 66*n*, 68*n*,
    69*n*, 73*n*, 93*n*
State of nature. *See* Nature, state of
States (nations)
  artificial division into, 41–42
  enmity between, 19, 20. *See also*
    War
  friendship among, 19–20
Stoicism, 12
Subordination. *See* Slavery;
    Tyranny
Sulla, Lucius Cornelius (Sylla),
    30–31
Superstition, 17
Sylla, 30–31

Tacitus, 34
Themistocles, 62
Theology (theologians), 83, 94, 95
  artificial, 78
Timotheus, 6*n*

Truth, 16–17
  suppression of, 59
Tyranny, 40, 42–56. *See also* Aristocracy; Despotism
  democracy as, 56, 57, 61–62
  ecclesiastical, 17, 18
  government as, 64, 92–93

Vandals, 34
Venice, 53, 65n
Vices, 73n, 93
*Vindication of Natural Society,
    A* (Burke)
  fictional form of, *xviii*, 9n

Vindication of Natural Society (cont.)
    publication of, *xxii–xxiii*
    as satire vs. serious tract, *xvi–
      xxii*, 4n, 36n
Virgil, 81n
Virtue, 16

War, 20–39, 42, 92, 94
Work. *See* Labor

Xerxes, 25–26

Zeno of Citium, 12n

The Palatino typeface used in this volume is the work of Hermann Zapf, the noted European type designer and master calligrapher. Palatino is basically an "old style" letterform, yet is strongly endowed with the Zapf distinction of exquisiteness. With concern not solely for the individual letter but also for the working visual relationship in a page of text, Zapf's edged pen has given this type a brisk, natural motion.

Book Design by JMH Corporation, Indianapolis, Indiana
Typography by Typoservice Corporation, Indianapolis, Indiana
Printed and Bound by Worzalla Publishing Co., Stevens Point, Wisconsin